Getting Past
"IF ONLY"

Getting Past
"IF ONLY"

KIM A. NELSON

Covenant Communications, Inc.

Cover image: *Freedom* © Xaviarnau, iStockphotography.com

Cover design copyright © 2011 by Covenant Communications, Inc.

Published by Covenant Communications, Inc.
American Fork, Utah

Printed in Canada
First Printing: September 2011

17 16 15 14 13 12 11   10 9 8 7 6 5 4 3 2 1

ISBN-13: 978-1-60861-459-2

For our friends John and Hollie Hansen

Acknowledgments

SPECIAL THANKS TO ALL WHOSE support and efforts have made this book a reality:

Rachel Johnson, my friend and teacher, who read, corrected, questioned, erased, underlined, and encouraged above and beyond the call of duty.

Emily Watts, my editor, whose only fault I have yet to find.

Kirk Shaw, at Covenant Book, who adopted me and made this project a reality with his support and willing editorial excellence.

Debbie Leavitt, who willingly discussed concepts and challenged ideas from the beginning.

Hilary and Tim Weeks and Emily and Greg Freeman, who provided a forum for group discussion early on in the process.

Thanks to all who took the time to read and comment on the work in progress:

Jane Pugh	Carlen Morland
Mark Middlesworth	Monique Martin
Jane Plank	Tanya Hudson
Cindy Rigtrup	Sherry Lowe
Kari and Pete Crossley	Heidi Werry

Finally, and most of all, thanks to my wife, Lois, who keeps believing in me.

Introduction: Getting Past "If Only"

I CAN TELL YOU THE exact moment, down to the year, month, day, and hour, that my friend Jim decided he would never be financially successful. To this day, every morning, Jim goes to the newspaper and makes a decision to be unhappy. He finds in the stock section of the paper the confirmation that he is not successful and never will be.

March 13, 1986, was the day Jim failed. That was the day Microsoft stock went public. Jim had $50,000 in his retirement account. It was a self-directed account, and he had the ability to choose where to invest that money. He had weighed the option of purchasing Microsoft stock; he liked the product, but there were other companies on the horizon that seemed to Jim to be more secure. Microsoft was a young company, and although it was doing well, it was experiencing some pending legal trouble with IBM and others. Jim decided that morning not to purchase Microsoft stock.

As it turned out, the stock took off and paid almost unimaginable dividends. It was one of the best stock opportunities in history. Jim decided as he watched the stock rise that his choice had doomed him. His decision not to purchase that stock had made his future financial situation forever a comparative failure. He had missed the boat. In his mind, he had missed the *only boat of all time.*

From that morning on March 13, 1986, to this very day, every single morning, without exception, the first thing Jim does is calculate what his Microsoft investment would have been worth. I can't tell you exactly what that investment of $50,000 would be worth now—certainly millions and millions of dollars. But I could call Jim and ask, and he would know . . . to the penny. He is ever aware of the exact magnitude of his failure.

For Jim, one decision became a lifetime of failure. Acutely conscious of what was "lost," Jim focused on "if only." His ongoing game of "if only" continued as Jim imagined all the things he would have purchased with his missed wealth. He showed me where the new pool would have been. He described in great detail his new airplane and the cabin in the Cascades he might have had. The imaginary money was immune to depletion. The value of his Microsoft stock never went down. That is the beauty of pretending: We can skip the laws of the real world and beat ourselves to death with what would have been, "if only."

Jim missed some very important details as he sat and stewed year after year. He had *lost* no money by not investing in Microsoft stock. In fact, his other investments had done fairly well. But his blind devotion to his mistake kept him from enjoying his real financial successes.

I don't believe the biggest loss Jim suffered was the lost income from a stock choice. The biggest loss was the loss of confidence, hope, strength, courage, and hours spent pining when he reviewed and wallowed each day in what he decided was his ultimate failure.

A hopeful vision of the future is what moves us forward. The adversary wants to keep us from those choices that would lead us to peace and happiness. He wants to distract us from the possibilities that our agency offers. One of the ways he does that is by convincing us that our past choices have made future success impossible. He wants to trap us in "if only."

Have you ever experienced the pain of regret? Have you ever revisited a past choice and asked yourself what could have been if only you had chosen differently? It's hard to avoid such feelings sometimes, and yet if we focus on the past, like my friend Jim, we can easily begin to lose confidence. We can get to a point where we don't trust ourselves to make good decisions.

It doesn't have to be that way. Our Savior wants great things for us, and He has offered us a partnership to create the best possible outcomes in this earthly testing ground. Remember, no one knows better than He does just how hard the world can be. Speaking to us as the lambs He loves, Jesus made his purposes clear: "The thief cometh not, but for to steal, and to kill, and to destroy: I am come that they might have life, and that they might have it more abundantly" (John 10:10).

Our role in the divine partnership with the Father and the Savior is to accept the gifts they give us and exercise them wisely and with faith. Our Father's wish for us is not just that we survive but that we flourish. Our best efforts, given our condition here, coupled with the gifts of agency, the Atonement, and the Holy Ghost, will not only get us safely home but also allow us to flourish here in mortality. That is what it means to have life and have it more abundantly. This is what it means to live free from regrets.

A life without *regret* is not the same thing as a life without *sorrow.* How many times have you heard a person say about a difficult time in his or her life, "In hindsight, it was worth it"? Perhaps you yourself have thought something like, "I'm not anxious to go through anything that hard again, but, looking back, it will always be a time I value because of what I learned."

Life will not be perfect, but it will be better if we choose well than if we choose poorly. We want to make it as good as it can be. We want the very best our lives can offer. So we need to learn to make wise choices and to concentrate on moving forward rather than looking back with regret.

The most powerful example I have ever seen of looking forward to an abundant life, rather than backward with a mind full of "if only" questions, came from a woman I met at a gathering where I was speaking. I don't even know her name, and I have never had the opportunity to thank her for being one of the most important teachers in my life.

The conference where I had spoken had come to an end. I was standing near the front of the auditorium when a lovely young woman in a wheelchair approached me. She introduced herself as a convert of about a year and expressed her thanks for the event. She asked me if I was a member of the Church. I assured her that I was. She asked if I held the Melchizedek Priesthood. I replied that I did. She then asked me if I was worthy to give a blessing. This caused me to pause and make a brief moral accounting in my mind, but after a moment, I said I was. She explained that she was staying with a non-LDS family, was a day and a half from home, and needed a blessing using consecrated oil. She assured me that she knew that her home teacher or bishop would have been the right person to ask for a blessing, but under the circumstances, I would have to do.

I asked her to wait briefly while I went to look for another Melchizedek Priesthood holder to help with the ordinance. It took only a minute to locate a friend who I knew was active and would be willing to help. We returned and asked the sister if we could find a little more appropriate place for the ordinance. We found a small room backstage that was quiet and out of the way. We had a brief prayer and asked her to tell us why she had sought the blessing.

I made brief notes later that night because her story had made such an impact on me. Although not verbatim, this is very close to what she said, based on my notes and memory. Please notice the time line of her situation.

She began by telling us that she had joined the Church about fourteen months earlier. Two months after her baptism, she was diagnosed with multiple sclerosis. Three months after that, her nonmember husband left without warning; she and her children were still not sure where he was. Her three boys—ages eight, seven, and five—all had significant challenges. The older boys had ADHD, and her five-year-old son was autistic. The pain from her MS and the lack of stability it caused forced her to use the wheelchair. To complicate her situation even further, she was very allergic to all pain medications except morphine. Her state-appointed child protective services caseworker told her that if she used morphine for the pain, the state would be required to put her boys in foster care.

After she finished this overwhelming story, which caused me to feel utter despair for what she was experiencing, she looked up at us and said, "Brethren, I need you to bless me that I can learn to love my new life." She then folded her arms, bowed her head, and waited for her blessing. We administered the blessing, and the sister thanked us and went peacefully on her way.

That woman's simple request changed my life. I have heard her words in my mind a thousand times since then as I have said my prayers or felt like too much was being asked of me. She showed me by her example what it looked like to trust God and trust in the Atonement. She really believed what the missionaries had taught her when she accepted the gospel. She believed what she read in the scriptures. She received the gift of faith that was promised as part of the baptismal covenant, and the gift of the Holy Ghost that accompanied it. She had chosen to live her life without dwelling on regret or "if only."

Did this sister have an easy life? Obviously not. She was in the midst of some very difficult challenges. But in the heart of this storm, she decided to exercise her agency and get the most out of the experience.

This woman could have been filled with bile about the decision her husband had made to leave her and the boys. It would be easy for anyone in her circumstances to justify feeling like a victim and seeing the world without hope. We have all seen people completely withdraw from the world and become bitter and consumed by negative feelings in similarly trying situations. But rather than being a victim, this woman chose to take an active role in building the best life possible. She refused to let her husband's betrayal destroy her trust in others or in God. She sought ways to deal with her pain rather than give in to it. She decided to learn all that she could, trust in the Lord, and try to learn to love her life.

There is a quote by Robert Lewis Stevenson that describes perfectly the peace I saw as this woman exercised her faith and agency. I have it hanging in my office, and I think of her every day when I read it: "Quiet minds cannot be perplexed or frightened, but go on in fortune or misfortune at their own private pace, like a clock during a thunderstorm."

Quiet minds come as a result of our taking an active and affirmative role in our own lives. Partnering with the Spirit as we go allows us to be less confused and scared. We then are able to move forward at our own pace toward experiencing life more abundantly.

This life is not about being perfect—an impossibility here in mortality for anyone but our Savior—but rather about becoming more and more like our Father. By understanding and applying the principles explored throughout this book, we can have more peace and feel closer to heaven as we continue to learn and love.

Section 1

Accepting the Gift of Agency

If we want to live with less regret, one of the things we need to do is take ownership of our lives. Taking responsibility allows us to make choices that will greatly increase our probability for happiness. We will see that we can be more involved in our own lives when we exercise our agency. We can make better decisions. We can heal from the sorrows and wounds we carry if we consciously choose to learn and grow from our experiences rather than waste time and energy on "if only." One way we move beyond regret and begin the journey is by *receiving the gift of agency.*

Accepting that we are gifted with the right and responsibility to choose is not always easy. We will all experience the feeling at some point in our lives that we are acted upon and have no way of influencing how things in our lives will turn out. It is true that there are some things over which we have no control. The death of a loved one, loss of employment because of downsizing, an illness such as cancer, a natural disaster—there are many such examples of things that we just can't control.

Elder Neal A. Maxwell taught, "Without our individual refining, . . . life would become merely a pass-through, audited course—not a course for credit. Only in the latter arrangement can our experiences and our performances be sanctified for our own everlasting good (see 2 Nephi 32:9). Mortality therefore is not a convenient, suburban, drive-around beltway with a view. Instead it passes slowly through life's inner city. Daily it involves real perspiration, real perplexity, real choosing, real suffering—and real refining!" (*If Thou Endure It Well* [Salt Lake City: Bookcraft, 1996], 8).

Events like these can make us feel as if we don't have the ability to choose what happens in our lives and, therefore, have no control over our destiny. No one is happier than the adversary when an individual feels out of control. He knows that this hopelessness can lead us to helplessness if it keeps us from exploring how to move forward. But even when outward circumstances are beyond our control, our capacity to make good choices remains.

Elder David A. Bednar beautifully describes the process of applying the gift of choice and our opportunity to use it:

> In the grand division of all of God's creations, there are things to act and things to be acted upon (see 2 Nephi 2:13–14). As sons and daughters of our Heavenly Father, we have been blessed with the gift of moral agency, the capacity for independent action and choice. Endowed with agency, you and I are agents, and we primarily are to act and not just be acted upon. To believe that someone or something can *make* us feel offended, angry, hurt, or bitter diminishes our moral agency and transforms us into objects to be acted upon. As agents, however, you and I have the power to act and to choose how we will respond to an offensive or hurtful situation ("And Nothing Shall Offend Them," *Ensign*, November 2006, 90).

Receiving the gift of agency begins by believing that we have been given a gift. We need to accept that we possess and can apply this gift that we were given in heaven. Agency is our right to make choices.

The Gift of Agency

We know from scripture and modern revelation that we had agency in the premortal existence. We used our agency while we were in the presence of our Heavenly Father. We had a chance to affirm Heavenly Father's confidence in us by supporting His plan of happiness. We were given the choice to come to earth, use our agency, and accept a Savior to make it possible for us to return to the presence of our Father. We also had the choice to accept and follow Satan's plan, which required restraints on our agency. We chose individually. Our mortal birth affirms the choice each of us made to come to earth to be tested as part of Heavenly Father's plan.

We knew what the earthly test would be like and what was at stake. We didn't make an uninformed choice to follow Heavenly Father; we had all the conditions of mortal life explained to us, as well as all the requirements to return to our Father. We know that we were not compelled to make this choice because many did not. Our brothers and sisters who followed the adversary *chose* not to come with us. Our response to their choice in heaven was just like it is here when a brother or sister makes a bad choice. It is recorded in D&C 76:26: We weep.

Choice is so vital a component to our becoming like our Father that Satan's insistence on keeping it from us was a huge factor in the war in heaven. The adversary believed we could not be trusted with such a powerful and important privilege. Our Father, on the other hand, has confidence in us. He wants us to learn and grow, and He knows that we can. This is why whenever we interact with our Heavenly Father, we have the opportunity to make choices.

The choices God gives us are always informed choices, even when it comes to Him. Father knew that if we were going to become more like Him, we had to experience the consequences of our choices.

When we receive the Father's gift of choice, it means that we accept responsibility for our choices and the subsequent consequences. As mentioned before, there is no such thing as a pain- or challenge-free life, because part of our earthly test involves dealing with challenges. The consequences of mortality are often painful. The important thing to remember is that when we exercise our agency and accept responsibility for our choices, we participate fully in our lives. We open the door to feel success and failure. Both teach us. Both give us the opportunity to learn, but only if we take responsibility.

Regardless of the circumstances we find ourselves in, there are decisions we can make that affect the outcomes in our lives. Being willing to accept that fact is a key to consciously moving toward living with less regret and fewer "if only" thoughts.

Influenced by Our Past

We often have difficulty identifying what parts of our lives we can and can't affect with our choices, and some of that confusion comes because of our experiences as children. Some of our childhood experiences teach us that we have little or no control over what happens in our lives. Almost everyone has been taught to believe in this powerlessness to some degree.

Some examples of how we are taught might sound like this:

"The world is not safe."

"You can't fight the government."

"That is who we are."

"Because I said so, that's why."

"Why must you always argue? Just do as you are told."

"Who do you think you are?"

Do any of those sound familiar?

Sometimes we are taught things that simply aren't true. Let me give you an example. Suppose that, from the time I was little, every time I saw an orange, everybody around me called it an apple. Naturally, I'm going to call it an apple because I don't know any differently. But eventually, I will end up somewhere where somebody will say, "No, that's an orange." I will then check enough credible sources to realize that I have been taught the wrong thing. That doesn't mean that the people who taught me knew that the apple was an orange and were just trying to mislead me. Most likely, they thought it was an apple.

The same holds true in far more important areas of our lives than fruit. If somebody says, "This is love," and if what I experience or see is painful, or humiliating, or demanding, or unreasonable, or unkind, that is what I'm going to call love. So at some point in my life, when people say I need to get married to experience great love, I say, "No thank you; I've had love, and it's nasty." I might believe, based on what I was taught, that whenever you love somebody, it hurts you.

There are myriad lies that I might believe because of the beliefs and mislabeling of those who taught me. For example:

"No man can be trusted."

"All women are whiners."

"One person really doesn't matter much."

"The higher your current Church position, the more righteous you are."

"God likes rich people best; that is why He blesses them with wealth."

While we review these examples, we've got to remember that even if we were taught the wrong thing, it doesn't mean that the intention of those who taught us was to hurt us. If we jump to that conclusion, not only do we do them a disservice but we also might cut ourselves off from people who care about us a great deal.

Many of the lessons we learned in life from others were based on what they did as much as what they said. They may have said, "God cares about you no matter what," but that was not what they showed us. If there was a withdrawal or hurtful criticism every time a mistake was made, the clear lesson from those who loved us was, "My acceptance of you is based on your performance." The message many of us received over and over was, "Do what I want or I won't be your friend, or be good to you, or be your mom or dad." Sometimes "what was said" and "what was done" were so far apart that the confusion and contradiction became paralyzing.

Becoming Victims

Perhaps the messages we got in our past about our powerlessness were not expressed in words only. We may have seen other people in our lives—parents, extended family members, or people in our community—give up hope and accept the role of the victim. We might assume by watching those around us that the pressure of life is too great and it is inevitable that we become victims.

For example, my friend Bill had been a successful home builder for many years when an unforeseen credit crisis led to the failure of his business. He became morose and pushed away all attempts to help him start again. His comments to all who would listen sounded like this: "Why try? Big banks and big government will just take everything you build. The little guy doesn't have a chance."

My friend would often tell his children that there was no hope of home ownership for their generation. "Why try?" he would say. "It is only a false dream that will break your heart in the end." He clearly felt powerless and preached that message continually.

But, despite his setbacks, Bill was not really powerless. Helplessness is not a given. The gift of agency is the gift of empowerment. We can exercise our choice and change our feelings of helplessness to faith.

There *are* real victims in our world—people who have been harmed or even destroyed by forces beyond their control. However, there are many others—probably including us at times—who for a myriad of reasons choose to see themselves as victims. Most of those reasons come down to some version of the following:

1. Being a victim is easier or less painful than my other options, or

2. I am not aware of any other options.

Let's look at an example of someone who accepted the role of victim. This good person just lived the script she was assigned in her youth and believed she really didn't have much choice in how her life turned out.

Over a period of several months, I met with a young woman we will call Susan. Susan appeared to all who knew her to be living a great life. She told me, however, that she felt empty. We discussed depression and determined that chemical depression was not the issue. Susan was sad and she was pretty clear about why.

Susan wanted to have a family but had not had that opportunity. She had slowly resigned herself over many years to her current feeling of emptiness and sense of loss. Her purpose in coming to see me was in essence to find out how to get over these feelings. After describing her life in detail, she summarized by saying, "This is the way my life is. I know that. How do I get over wanting something I can't have?"

Let me paint a picture of Susan, as I experienced her. She was a wonderful young woman. She had a very good education and a responsible job with a stable company. She was beautiful and bright. She had been the prom queen at her high school, as well as class valedictorian. In her early thirties, she owned her own home and traveled extensively. She was an active person who loved to bike and snowboard. Susan had made good life choices and had stayed active in the Church. She came from a family of good people who were well-intentioned and loved her.

In our subsequent meetings, she continued to express real disappointment that she was unable to find an eternal companion. This disappointment seemed to be at the core of why she was feeling so negative and emotionally listless. What concerned me most was that she expressed little hope for change. No matter how she and I tried to infuse some hope into her life, she had the lingering belief that somehow living in a happy and positive marriage was impossible for her. The thing she wanted most was simply not in the cards—not *her* cards, anyway.

We talked about marriage and explored what the possibilities of a happy married life were for others. Was there such a thing, or was it a fairy tale? What would it look like? She wasn't sure.

She had watched her mom and dad over the years and realized that there was no spark in that marriage. She dreamed of a marriage partnership full of passion and real zest for living. She had always questioned whether marriage would be the joy that her Church leaders and others had always told her it was. That was not what she had seen. It was, however, what she wanted desperately if it existed.

That was not all. Her mother had pointed out to her and others on numerous occasions that she was the smart one in the family, or the pretty one, not the domestic one. She was not the one who would be good wife or mother material.

In fact, at one point, her mom made the offhand comment that it was too bad the practice of polygamy was no longer acceptable because Susan could not manage on her own, but as a second wife, her shortcomings would be less of a problem as she learned what was needed to be a good mom and make a man happy. This unintended insult influenced Susan's belief that she could never succeed as a wife and mother.

When Susan shared this story with me, she concluded it by saying, "I think my mom was right. I am just not wife material." She had taken this untrue message to heart and really believed it.

We discovered that whenever Susan got too close to what might be a successful relationship, she found a way to end it. She would always find a way to avoid the risk and shame of failure. By avoiding connection, she also escaped the grim possibility that she might end up in a relationship that would be eternally joyless.

After hearing her story, I asked Susan a simple question: "Is it possible that what you have chosen to believe about yourself and your opportunity for eternal happiness is wrong?"

She had come to believe so completely that she was destined to fall short and be alone that she was unable to respond to the question.

I asked the same question in a different way: "Can you look at your life experience and see any evidence that a positive marriage is possible for you?"

Still there was no response. So I continued our exchange by asking, "Susan, did you have friends as you grew up?" She replied that she had lots of friends. She said she was happy in social settings of every kind. She loved being with her friends and their families. She was often invited to go on trips with those families. Susan also had siblings whom she was close to, and she loved being around them, too.

"Susan, thinking back," I said, "did you ever observe the marriages of other people whom you knew—your friends' parents, for example? Was there any observable passion for life and real appreciation for each other in any of those marriages?"

As she considered the question, she concluded that there were plenty of those examples. She recalled a great number of advisers, teachers, and parents of close friends who did seem to be happy in their marriages. I asked her, even though her mom and dad had their kind of marriage, was it possible that much more was available for her and others? Was the level of passion she wanted in her life possible for her if she changed her expectations? Did her life experience demonstrate that she was capable of other, more desirable possibilities?

She pondered the question and realized that most of her life experience was in stark contrast to the picture she had painted of herself in her mind. Susan acknowledged that there were things she was very passionate about. She loved snowboarding, wakeboarding, mountain biking, and skiing. She loved to be outdoors. She loved music and the company of good people. These things gave her that sense of wellness and aliveness she wanted. She had been very successful in non-romantic relationships. It was at this point of self-discovery that she began to have some hope.

As we talked, she realized that she could translate her desire to be a successful wife and mother into reality—that she was actually very well-prepared for both the role of wife and that of mother. The belief that she was somehow doomed to fail was based on her unquestioning acceptance of poor information. She learned that she could trust her own experience and feel the influence of wise teachers and friends.

Susan's biggest problem was that she had accepted as reality the insights and labels of someone for whom marriage and mothering was not a passionate experience. Was her mom to blame? No. Even the best of intentions are sometimes flawed. It is up to us to learn what possibilities our lives hold, and by observing and experiencing for ourselves, we can be taught. We get to choose what to believe and how to respond. That is a gift from God. Our Father intended for us to learn by exercising choice. Susan chose to change her thinking. We can exercise our agency and make positive life changes no matter how flawed our picture of ourselves appears. The toughest experiences and bumpiest roads are often our motivation to ask the best questions and find the best answers.

By accepting responsibility for our choices, we stop being victims. If we are in a mud hole, we need to recognize one of the possible reasons for being there might be that we simply chose to be in a mud hole. Once we acknowledge that possibility, we are free to learn. We can then choose a response to our mud-hole experience.

When we choose the role of victim, the desire to abdicate our agency is everywhere. We incorporate our victim status into even our most commonly expressed feelings and think nothing of it. Here are some examples:

He made me mad.

She drives me crazy.

I can't take it anymore.

In other words, "My behavior is your fault." Or, perhaps even more to the point, "My behavior is not my fault."

What if we recognized that we really do have a choice? What might our responses in the very same situations look like?

"He made me mad" becomes "He behaved poorly, and I decided to do the same."

"She drives me crazy" could be "She does things that could irritate me if I chose to be irritated by them."

"I can't take it anymore" is simply "I have decided to throw a tantrum."

These are simple examples to be sure, but they make the point. One might argue that there are a lot of really bad things that happen to people over which they had no control. That may be true. We must not confuse choice with control. We can't control everything that happens to us, but we can control how we respond to what happens to us.

Just a caveat here: Physical and mental challenges may render some of God's children unaccountable for their actions. But it is very important to note that no matter what the challenges are in a person's life, those challenges don't give that person the right to abuse. We leave final judgment to God but always recognize that an unsafe environment is never what the Father would want us to be in. In any case of abuse, we have been counseled to seek safety for and to protect the innocent. Judging the level of accountability required of any of God's children is up to God. He will be loving and merciful in that decision like the perfect Father He is.

Accepting our gift of agency allows us to review our choices and our motives more closely. This acceptance turns "the devil made me do it" into "it looked like fun, and I decided to do what the adversary wanted me to." The latter is a tougher pill to swallow by far. Even though not all foolish choices are actually sins, I think we can all agree that the devil is happy when we choose poorly. When I recognize that my action was *my* choice, I gain the power to choose to change. The adversary never wants us to feel that empowered.

Learning to accept our choices and the fact that we have the ability to choose are what a life without regret is all about. Our purpose here on the earth is to learn to be more like our Father. He has given us the gift of agency to make that possible. Our agency is central to our happiness.

Accepting the Gift of Agency

Have you ever given someone a gift on Christmas morning, looked in the eyes of the person you gave it to, and known by that person's reaction that the gift was exactly right? In my experience, that's the best feeling of all. On the other hand, have you ever given somebody a gift and known that he or she was disappointed? That can be devastating. It is very disappointing to have a gift rejected by someone you were trying to please.

Picture this: After we pass through the veil into mortality, Heavenly Father leaves agency wrapped up under the tree and waits to see our faces as we open it. He wants to see us use it and enjoy it. Isn't it fun when someone loves the gift you have given so much that he or she can't wait to try it out? And it's even more fun when the person gets really good at using it!

How would it feel if you wrapped a present and the person you gave it to just left it under the tree? The lights get taken down, then the tree, and there sits your gift. You check, and sure enough, it has a tag on it. The gift is clearly marked and available to be claimed. So you wait. Do you think Heavenly Father ever sees that happen with His precious gift of agency?

There are many reasons we might give for not opening the gift of agency. For example, we might think, "I don't deserve that gift" or "Someone made a mistake. That couldn't possibly be for me." Maybe we choose not to unwrap it because we think it will mean more responsibility or an opportunity for more guilt. Maybe we're afraid that the gift isn't what we asked for and will be too hard to use. Does our unwillingness or fear make it a bad gift? Of course not. Our poor choice not to accept the gift is irrelevant. The gift is precious regardless.

Let me share an example of the impact of knowing I get to choose in my life. My mom is eighty-six years old. If I go to take her to dinner or a movie because she lives alone and I really love her, then we have a fun time. But if I go to take her to dinner and a movie because I don't want her to tell my brother and two sisters that I'm a no-good son, it's a completely different experience in how it nourishes us both—or fails to. The very same activity can be experienced completely differently depending on why I do it. In any activity, it is better to choose than it is to feel forced or obligated.

Visiting or home teaching is another common experience that is affected profoundly by why we choose to do it.

Sometimes I avoided going home teaching like it were a trip to the dentist. It must be done, but only after as much delay as possible.

I realized one day after a particularly enjoyable experience that there is a pattern to my home teaching. Even though sometimes I resist it, every time I go, I enjoy it. I don't just tolerate it or feel relief that it's over; I enjoy it. I have shared my pattern with many people over the years who feel the same way. I think it was the thought of being assigned that can be hard to accept. Choosing to go home teaching because I love the people I visit changes the experience completely. I experience going to check in on a friend in a much more positive way than being forced to do a duty. The visit itself is the same, but I can choose to see it differently.

How we feel about God's gift of agency and His intentions toward us depends a lot on what we have been taught about Him. Does He really give gifts—or just assignments? Is He the kind of father who is just waiting for us to goof up so He can punish us? Is He really giving us a present or just another list of restrictions? Is God's voice one of concern or control? How did we learn about God? How can we know if we are right or wrong about Him?

Examining how we learned about God is vital if we are to understand why we feel the way we do about our relationship to Him. Is He kind? Is He interested in our success or failure? Can we really talk to Him, and does it matter?

In most cases, the people who taught us how to be adults taught us about God. It might have been our parents who taught us. Certainly for many of us, they had the most influence. However, grandparents, extended family members, significant neighbors, teachers, and friends all contributed to our learning. When we think of these people, it is important to remember that we can't know what the intent of their heart was when they taught us. Because we can't read their minds, we can only guess how they felt. So the best thing to do is to assume that their intent was positive. They were giving us the very best of what they had to give. Does that mean that it was useful or effective? Does the fact that they believed something make it right? No. That's why it's important to remember that we can't accurately evaluate the condition of their hearts or their intent. It is absolutely necessary, however, to be aware of and evaluate the *influence* of their teaching on our lives. We must understand that it had an impact and that some of it was likely negative.

For example, many of us have been taught by our experience that powerful people in our lives can't be trusted because those who were supposed to care for us did not. We depended on them, they were powerful to us, and they let us down. Because God is powerful, our experience would thus lead us to believe that He must not be benevolent. It doesn't seem possible that He could love us. As a result, we think God's love must be some kind of trick.

It is my personal belief that most of the people who taught us were genuinely giving us the best that they had to give. It is very important to remember, however, that if they were unknowingly giving us poison, we got poison.

So how do we find out for ourselves that God's gifts are good? We must experiment and see what we learn. This is well illustrated in one of my favorite Bible stories—when Andrew and Philip meet Christ for the first time. They were disciples of John the Baptist. It was John who suggested that they listen to the Savior.

They heard Him speak and were overwhelmed. They wanted to know more about Him, so they followed Him. Jesus realized they were following and asked them, "What seek ye?" To me, it seems that they were a little surprised by His question. They asked Him, "Where dwellest thou?" They were curious and wanted to get to know more about Him. His answer to them was loving and straightforward: "Come and see." And they did. What they found when they followed Him was so wonderful that they stayed with Him (John 1:38–39).

Andrew and Philip were curious. They wanted to know the nature of the Savior. So they chose to go and be with him. This experiment in faith changed their lives. They planted a seed to see what would grow, as described in Alma 32:27–28:

> But behold, if ye will awake and arouse your faculties, even to an experiment upon my words, and exercise a particle of faith, yea, even if ye can no more than desire to believe, let this desire work in you, even until ye believe in a manner that ye can give place for a portion of my words.
>
> Now, we will compare the word unto a seed. Now, if ye give place, that a seed may be planted in your heart, behold, if it be a true seed, or a good seed, if ye do not cast it out by your unbelief, that ye will resist the Spirit of the Lord, behold, it will begin to swell within your breasts; and when you feel these swelling motions, ye will begin to say within yourselves—It must needs be that this is a good seed, or that the word is good, for it beginneth to enlarge my soul; yea, it beginneth to enlighten my understanding, yea, it beginneth to be delicious to me.

That is what we need to do with His gift of agency. Accepting the gift of agency requires that we have the faith to experiment. We have to participate willingly. We need to act. We are not victims, unworthy or unable to make decisions for ourselves. We need to unwrap the gift of agency and see what it is in order to learn and grow. Can we really choose? Does Heavenly Father trust us that much? How can we be sure? It may seem too good to be true, based on our past life experience and perceptions. We need to go with the Savior and see, as did Andrew and Philip. What we will find will be so delicious that we will not want to leave.

When we truly know the Son, we know the Father. The better we come to know them, the more comfortable we become with our journey to be more like them. Knowing the Father and the Son connects us to our loving and caring eternal family and to each other as nothing else can. Our personal commitment to a relationship with our Father in Heaven will help us understand His commitment to us. He gave us the gift of agency because He loves us and wants us to learn. Everything we receive from Father begins with His love for us.

God's love allows us to bless ourselves and others with our choices. He has confidence in our ability to learn from our experiences. Satan would like us to perceive love differently. Satan wants us to believe that we can be loved only when we do what we are told or perform up to someone else's expectations perfectly.

I was raised in the Upper Snake River Valley in Idaho. In the process of growing up, I was infected with a very painful illness. I have found in my experience that many of the people raised in that area were similarly afflicted with that disease, which I call the Upper Snake River valley flu. I have since discovered that the disease is not as localized as I thought. It might as easily be called Cache Valley consumption or Dixie fever. Here are the symptoms: No matter what the question is, the answer is always, "Work harder." If there is anything in the world that is not going perfectly, it means you are not doing enough. You can't ask for help or you are weak.

When I suffer from this malady, over and over and over, whenever anything is going wrong, I just work harder. I don't take the time to stop and ask, "Am I maybe doing the wrong thing?" or "Why isn't this effective?" I just work harder. Every problem is my fault because somehow my effort was not good enough to fix the problem. So, for example, if I've got kids who make bad choices, I didn't work hard enough as a parent. If things aren't working out for me, the solution is not about changing or learning—the whole problem is that I'm just not doing enough. Much of the time, it feels like I am not trying hard enough to qualify for success, or respect, or even love. That includes God's love.

One of my favorite quotes has often been attributed to Abraham Lincoln: "The only thing worse than doing something poorly is doing the wrong thing well." And in our lives, unfortunately, when it comes to teaching us principles of problem-solving and self-esteem, some people do the wrong thing very well.

Believing that hard work, perfection, and a host of other things are required in order for us to earn God's love is wrong. That belief is the counterfeit of love promoted by Satan.

God's love for us and the gift of agency are the two things that fuel His plan. I really believe that's true. He honors us by giving us the chance to choose so we can learn and grow and have a positive effect on those around us. His way always begins "because He loves us."

If I make a mistake under Heavenly Father's plan, I say, "Oh no, I've made a mistake. I'm so sorry. Heavenly Father knew I wasn't going to be perfect—that is why His plan provided a Savior. What I know for sure is that He loves me and has confidence in me. I'm going to try again and move forward if I can. I will learn from this experience and do better. I will apply the Atonement to my life, and it will work."

The adversary's way, on the other hand, sounds like this: "If you do what you're told, you'll be loved." So if I make a mistake under that plan, I think, "Oh, I failed again. I'm never going to be good enough. I can't qualify. I'll never make it." We are filled with fear and self-hatred, and every single imperfection reinforces our feeling of being hopeless.

The reason the adversary lies is because he doesn't want us to understand that we can choose to learn from our mistakes and begin again. He wants us to believe that in our failure to measure up, we have disqualified ourselves from receiving God's affection. In fact, the gospel teaches us that even when we are at our very worst, God loves us. God's love for us is not a prize to be gained by our perfect performance or to be purchased with specific actions. His love is a gift that has been ours from the beginning and will always be.

The Agency of Others

Recognizing that the gift of agency is given to all of God's children can be difficult. Sometimes it would be much easier just to take responsibility ourselves for the actions of someone we love rather than to accept that he or she must take the consequences. For example, it is much easier for a mom or a dad to take the blame than to acknowledge the poor choices of a child. We love our children so much that we are often the last to see a pattern of poor choices or sin.

Have you ever considered statements like the following to be ways in which parents might actually try (probably unknowingly) to take agency away from their children?

"If we had been better at holding family home evenings, he would have stayed morally clean."

"I told you that you weren't having enough father's interviews."

"I know I could have done something more—I just don't know what it could have been."

Sometimes we try to blame the theft of our children's agency on others. For example:

"That Lyle Scott is just no good. If Jim hadn't been with him, he wouldn't have made any of those bad choices."

"I know my daughter, and she wouldn't do that. It's that boy."

Believe me, I know from personal experience how hard it can be when children stray. And in truth, the friend or the date may have had some influence. One fact remains, though: Our kids still had a choice. We *all* have a choice about our good and bad decisions. Sometimes even the best among us make bad decisions. We sin. When we make destructive choices, there is another choice to be made: Do we keep going down that path, or do we choose to change? In the case of sin, we can confess and abandon the sin, then begin again more intelligently and make better choices this time. And our children, our friends, and our loved ones can do the same thing.

What we choose defines us and prepares us to learn. The gift of agency is the very heart of our earthly existence. In the great council in heaven, God declared His intention to see if we would choose to follow Him: "And we will prove them herewith, to see if they will do all things whatsoever the Lord their God shall command them" (Abraham 3:25). It takes patience and faith to afford others the opportunity to undergo this proving for themselves.

Consider, for example, Sue and Rob, parents who were determined to see their children succeed in school. Their commitment to this worthwhile goal went beyond the normal and appropriate assistance that most parents provide. They would badger teachers for better grades for their children, take over a large part of the responsibility for getting the homework done (in the name of "helping"), and decide what activities the children would be involved in to maximize their chances of getting into good universities. Were their children allowed to own those choices? Do you suppose they felt responsible for the consequences? How much power do you think they felt in their own lives?

If, by contrast, those kids had made the choice themselves to better their grades at school, that choice would acknowledge that—to some degree, at least—what grades they got were up to them. That choice would open the door to feeling satisfaction when their efforts paid off with an improved grade.

In my own life, choosing to serve a mission was one of the best choices I have ever made. The blessings that have come to me as a result of that choice are almost immeasurable. That experience opened the door to everything that followed. I was not pressured to go on a mission, and knowing that the choice was mine alone was a great gift. It was a tremendous confidence builder to know not only that I could make good choices but also that I could finish what I started.

Just as we need to allow others to take responsibility for their own choices, we need to allow ourselves to be accountable and not fall into the trap of being too concerned about what others think. When we base our choices on what we think will win us the most approval, we may surrender some of our agency. William Jordan put it quite nicely: "Being hypersensitive to the opinions others have of us puts us into the false position of making their approval our court of appeals instead of our own conscience and self-respect."

One day, a letter came to our stake president from a member of the singles ward in our area. I was a member of the stake presidency, and the letter—signed, "a concerned member"—contained several comments about me. "When President Nelson stands up to speak, the Spirit leaves the room," it said. The writer believed that I was too light-minded in a specific meeting where the bishop had asked me to bear my testimony. In that testimony, I had chided the brethren of the Melchizedek Priesthood in what I thought was a loving and lighthearted way. I suggested that the men of the singles ward were not honoring their priesthood if they were not worthy and ready to give blessings or go to the temple. I asked how they could expect to marry in the temple, assuming they were lucky enough to trick some worthy sister into marrying them, if they were not holding a current temple recommend. I'm sure that was not all I said, but that is what I remember.

Surprisingly enough, after that same meeting, I got a note and the stake president got a phone call, both from men who said they realized they had some corrections to make and would do better. But that "concerned member" had experienced my remarks completely differently—had decided that I was flippant, that I had no right to be critical, and that I was self-aggrandizing.

As you can imagine, that letter hurt me. I took it, read it carefully, and returned it to the stake president. I went to the temple that week and asked Heavenly Father what I should do. Had I pushed too hard? Had I phrased things inappropriately? It was my responsibility to review my behavior, learn from it, and improve.

It is the responsibility of the hearer to listen and get the message in a meeting and choose what to do with it. Writing a concerned letter in this case was one person's choice; dropping a note and making a phone call were two others. The point is that how we respond is up to us. How I react to criticism or praise is up to me. No one has the power to make me feel offended, but I certainly can choose to be.

Understanding Our Blessings

It is hard to know sometimes which of our experiences are blessings and which are not. How many times have you said or heard someone else say that a difficult experience, looking back, was worth it? I have heard the opposite as well—many times what looked at first like a blessing turned into a nightmare. We have all seen marriages (or been in them) that had a tough spot or two. Some marriages have thrived against all odds, while others that looked at first like a fairy tale have crumbled.

This goes to show that we can't always tell how things will turn out. When we choose, we must accept the consequences of our choices and make the best of what we learn.

Unfortunately, we see people around us who are filled with bile; trouble follows them all the time. These are the people who are working the hardest to give agency back. They don't have any confidence in God's faith in us. They somehow think all is lost before it even begins.

Here is a story that reminds us that sometimes adversity is a blessing in disguise:

Long ago, King's Law made it legal for a man to be abducted and pressed into naval service against his will. The hero of our story was waylaid and forced to go to sea on a sailing ship. He was locked in the lower hold of the ship. He was sure things couldn't get worse.

Then the ship ran into a terrible storm. "Things just got worse," he thought. The ship's cargo was wood for shipbuilding. When the ship broke apart in the storm, the man was saved by clinging to the wood that made up the cargo.

Morning found him alive but floating alone in the ocean. He was sure things couldn't get worse. That evening, after only a few hours, a friendly current washed him up on a deserted island.

The next morning, he climbed a small hill near where he had landed. What he saw from the hill convinced him that things couldn't get worse. He was on a tiny island, and there was no other land in sight. "Oh, great," he thought. "I will die alone on a deserted island."

It began to rain, and he realized that without shelter, all was lost. He had no way of making shelter. In despair, he just crawled into the jungle and slept. Things had become worse yet.

When he walked around the island the next day, he found a chest that had washed up on the beach. In the chest were tools, a few matches, and a blanket. He worked every day over the next weeks to build his shelter. He had fire for warmth and would soon have a roof over his head.

When at last his new home was completed, he moved in. That first night in his new home, the fire in the fire pit got out of control as he slept, waking him just barely in time to save his life. All else was lost. "I think I should just kill myself" was his last thought before he fell into an exhausted sleep.

He awoke to the sound of voices. There was a longboat on the beach and a military schooner in the bay. A young officer introduced himself and said that they had been blown off course. They were well out of any shipping lanes. "Even at that, we almost missed this little island," he said. "It is not on any of our charts. You are a lucky man. If it had not been for your signal fire last night, you may never have been found."

The shipwrecked man said a silent prayer for the good fortune of his burned shelter.

As we learn from that story, adversity is sometimes a blessing. But the blessing in adversity can be hard to see, depending on our perspective. I can't tell you how many times, as a bishop, I heard things like, "I did everything right, and Heavenly Father will not heal my son / force my daughter to quit dating that guy / make my dad quit drinking." My own father was an alcoholic, and it was really hard some days. I would bargain with Heavenly Father, saying things like, "I'll give you a thousand hours if you'll make my dad stop drinking." God didn't do it when I wanted him to; He was not on my timetable. I had my agency to believe or not to believe that God was hearing my prayers. My father also had agency to stop drinking—which he eventually did, by the way. His sobriety and Church activity at the end of his life are a real tribute to his faith and his choice.

I missed the point of agency by trying to compel God by my actions to give me certain blessings. I was familiar with the scripture: "And when we obtain any blessing from God, it is by obedience to that law upon which it is predicated" (D&C 130:21). I was under the impression at the time that all I had to do was figure out which law matched which blessing and obey it, and God would be compelled to bless me: "I, the Lord, am bound when ye do what I say . . ." (D&C 82:10). So if I'm just obedient, I get everything. If I don't get something I want, it must mean that in some way, I have been disobedient.

One problem with this thinking is that it assumes we understand perfectly when we are being blessed. As we have already observed, blessings may come in forms that we don't readily recognize. The Lord may be bound to bless us, but He is not required to do so in the manner that we prescribe.

One of my favorite Taoist parables helps illustrate that we can't always predict what is or isn't a blessing, but we can choose how we respond to our circumstances.

There was an old farmer who had worked his crops for many years. One day, his horse ran away. Upon hearing the news, his neighbors came to visit. "Such bad luck," they said sympathetically.

"Maybe," the farmer replied.

The next morning, the horse returned, bringing with it three other wild horses. "How wonderful!" the neighbors exclaimed.

"Maybe," replied the old man.

The following day, his son tried to ride one of the untamed horses, was thrown, and broke his leg. The neighbors again came, this time to offer their sympathy on his son's misfortune. "How terrible," they said.

"Maybe," replied the farmer.

The next morning, military officials came to the village to draft young men into the army. Seeing that the son's leg was broken, they passed him by. The neighbors congratulated the farmer on how well things had turned out.

"Maybe," said the farmer.

When we judge too quickly or without the appropriate perspective, we make all kinds of mistakes about what blessings are and what those apparent blessings mean. We jump to conclusions that don't quite work. Consider this train of logic:

1. It's a good thing, a blessing, to have a cabin or vacation home for your family.

2. Heavenly Father blesses the righteous.

3. Therefore, if I have a cabin or a vacation home, it is proof that I'm righteous—and if you don't have a cabin, you must not be righteous.

Name anything that could be construed as a blessing. A singing voice or the gift of musical talent could be the blessing we want. In some cases, the ability to have children would top the list. Many times, monetary blessings or prestige in our community or profession are the blessings we seek.

Since God gives blessings to the righteous, it seems to follow that if I don't have those desired blessings, I'm not as righteous as someone who does. Now, doctrinally, we know that doesn't make sense, but emotionally, depending on how we are feeling about our Father in Heaven, it can make perfect sense. If we have been taught that love is something we have to earn, it isn't too far a leap to believe that blessings are earned as well. We need to remember that we don't earn all the blessings we have. Many are simply gifts from a loving Father. And many things that look like blessings may not really be what we need most. The greatest blessing is to become like our Heavenly Father.

Elder David A. Bednar taught us about this principle of Father's gifts in this way: "We may falsely think that such blessings and gifts are reserved for other people who appear to be more righteous or who serve in visible Church callings. I testify that the tender mercies of the Lord are available to all of us and that the Redeemer of Israel is eager to bestow such gifts upon us" ("The Tender Mercies of the Lord," *Ensign*, May 2005, 101).

We can demonstrate our appreciation for those gifts by gratefully accepting the kindness of a loving Father.

It is natural to want to know how everything is going to turn out. I am not sure if it is because I am curious or afraid, but I feel that way. For now, though, we can't always know what is going to happen in our lives. What we *can* know is that we can control how we respond to what comes our way. Experiment with me. Try responding consciously to life's challenges and joys, with faith that our Father sees and knows what is happening to us and rejoices in our ability to choose wisely.

A Native American friend of mine asked me if I really believed in a loving and benevolent Father in Heaven, as I had told him. I said I did.

"Then in the end, it will all be okay. Is that right?" he asked.

"Yes," I replied.

"So calm down. If it is not all right, it is not the end."

I testify that God is the very best example of all things good. The effective use of choice is no exception. He chooses to love us. He chooses to let us grow from our experiences. God honors our agency by inviting, not compelling. He gives the gift of love to us without any guarantee that we will love Him in return. He has given us the gift of agency knowing full well that many of us won't accept it.

The process of owning our choices is, paradoxically, one of both self-empowerment and humility. We accept accountability for our decisions while at the same time acknowledging God's gift to and support of us. He has faith in us and upholds us in exercising our will. He knows we will not be perfect, and He knows we will learn. As we accept the gift of agency, we can lay aside regrets and "if onlys" and know the joy of becoming more like Him.

Section 2

Setting Healthy Boundaries

All of us have had some sort of pain in our lives. We don't like it. One of our common responses to pain is to try to find a place where it will be impossible for us to be hurt again. Understanding and applying reasonable boundaries in our lives helps us overcome past hurts and the paralysis and fear of the future that those hurts produce.

Gerald Lund wrote, "The heart is a tender place. It is sensitive to many influences, both positive and negative. It can be hurt by others. It can be deadened by sin. It can be softened by love. Early in our lives, we learn to guard our hearts. It is like we erect a fence around our hearts with a gate in it. No one can enter that gate unless we allow him or her to" ("Opening Our Hearts," *Ensign*, May 2008).

Many of our deepest hurts come from our relationships. Appropriate boundaries help us make better choices about where and with whom we are safe. Setting appropriate boundaries helps us avoid possible future pain, giving us a better chance of experiencing a life without regret.

Making and maintaining effective boundaries requires us to have confidence in ourselves and in our choices. We need to be able to trust our ability to identify those people or circumstances that are potentially hurtful. And yet, after we have been hurt, it becomes more difficult to trust ourselves. After all, we weren't very good at it before or we wouldn't have been hurt.

We want to fully embrace every opportunity to get all the learning and love possible out of our lives. At the same time, we want to be safe from hurt. This seeming dichotomy leaves us with the question of how to build the confidence required to interact with others and our world in the safest possible way.

Once we have been hurt, we know it is possible to be hurt. That changes us. We are ever after on the lookout. This is especially true when the person who hurts us is a person who we believed was supposed to be kind, to protect us, to love us. That is why hurting a child is so devastating to that child's ability to develop trust in the future.

An all-too-common coping strategy for avoiding the future pain of betrayed trust might sound like this: "In order to keep from being hurt again by someone I love, I won't love anyone." Or, similarly: "If I never trust anyone, I will never be let down by someone I trust again."

Such an attitude presents two real problems. Problem one is that this coping strategy works perfectly. If I never trust or love, I will never be let down by someone I trust or love. If there is no one around, there is no one to cause pain. Problem two is that when I isolate myself from relationships, the cure is more damaging than the disease. It would be like curing a hangnail by cutting off my finger. True, I wouldn't have the hangnail, but it is easy to see that this solution is overkill.

The Parable of the Car Door

I am not saying that the hurt and pain of feeling betrayed is equivalent to the pain of a hangnail. It is not a little thing to be hurt or feel let down. I am saying, however, that not loving or not trusting, when taken to the extreme, is as devastating to our souls as amputation is to our bodies. Not trusting or loving leaves us alone, empty, and bitter. Perhaps I can best illustrate by an example that I call "The Parable of the Car Door."

Let's say I take a friend out to the car, open the door, and ask him to put his hand in the opening. When he does so, I slam the door really hard on his hand, breaking bones and ripping flesh. I then open the door, bandage the hand, set the bones, and stitch it up as required. Afterward, I ask him to put his hand in the door a second time. He'll probably say something like, "What kind of idiot do you take me for?" That seems like a reasonable response to my request. I don't think I would exhibit trust either if I were in the same situation.

The difficulty comes when we interpret the car door experience wrongly. We may generalize that experience and apply it to everyone and every car. We begin to see all cars as potential pain-givers. Pretty soon, we don't want to go near a car. We don't even want to live near a road or where we can hear a car. We could even say that car doors are the problem, forgetting that it was the person—not the car door—who hurt us.

This coping strategy works perfectly. If we never go near cars, we never have our hand slammed in the door again. But if we stay away from cars, we can never go to the airport and catch a flight to Hawaii. We can't visit our kids and grandkids. We can't see and do all of those beautiful things that riding in cars allows us to do.

When someone causes us pain, we might generalize and say that relationships are the problem. If we're afraid of all relationships, like being afraid of all cars, we've missed the point. It is true that the car door can hurt us—relationships and love can hurt us. In reality, the real problem is not about relationships; it is about the person with whom we choose to be in the relationship. But sometimes we isolate ourselves from relationships rather than risk learning how to choose better door-holders.

Learning to choose well helps us develop the confidence that we can be better at discerning who can be trusted. That confidence will make the risk of reaching out to others seem less ominous.

A Bag of Cats

Our life experiences shape our perspective. Our view of the past colors how we see the world today. It is understandable, then, that past experiences have significant impact, positively and negatively, on our current perceptions.

A therapist friend shared a story with me that illustrates how our past experiences might affect our responses in the present. She was driving down a country road and observed a man throwing a bag from his truck. She noticed that the bag was moving and pulled over to see what was inside. As an animal lover, she was horrified to realize that the bag contained several young cats. The man was obviously trying to get rid of what he saw as a problem. The cats were agitated and frightened beyond belief. My friend was worried that being tossed from a moving vehicle might have injured them. In an effort to reassure them and assess the damage, she opened the bag. She quickly discovered that the cats were not aware of her benevolent motivation. Rather than being reassured and calmed by a friendly face, they became even more agitated. They did everything in their power to escape from the bag and their experience in it. They lashed out in an effort to defend themselves from what they perceived to be a continuation of the threat to their safety.

With some effort and a good deal of pain, my friend managed to keep the cats in the bag. The best thing she could think to do was get them to a veterinarian. The cats were cared for, provided with food, and given a safe shelter.

Knowing that the cats were safe, my friend took a moment to reflect on her experience. She realized that the cats had no way of knowing her intention as she opened the bag. In fact, based on their experience, their best bet was that the person who held the bag was most likely out to hurt them. Their action was more instinctive than thoughtful.

This story caused me to reflect on the assumptions I make as I communicate with others. It was easy to see a parallel between the bag of cats and many of the people I had tried to help over the years. Unfortunately, many of us have had life experiences that have given us the impression that we can expect no gentleness, kindness, or protection from others. In fact, we may have learned to expect quite the opposite from those we interact with. Based on our experiences, we assume that interactions with others will inevitably be painful. So it is only reasonable that, in an effort to protect ourselves, we respond like the cats did. If we equate human interaction with pain, we will strive to find almost any means to avoid it.

The lesson we learn here doesn't apply only to those who have been seriously abused or have suffered greatly. Even seemingly small things can have lasting consequences in our lives. I have spent much of my adult life working with construction workers and managers. Many of the people who enter the trades do so because they are not comfortable in the classroom. The thought of college is just too painful. The foremen and managers I have worked with are very bright and capable. Most love to read and are always ready to learn on the job. They are good with people and have excellent organizational skills. I observed this phenomenon for years and wondered why the thought of school was difficult for so many.

One of my responsibilities was management training. I began asking those who expressed a resistance to the classroom why they felt negatively about this kind of learning. Almost without exception, the answers I got sounded something like this:

"When I was in elementary school, one of my teachers told the class what a poor student I was. I never liked school after that. After all, I was not going to be successful, so why try?"

"I was in the dumb reading group. Everyone knows that the kids in my family are not good students. We are blue-collar people, not college people."

No matter what the perceived roadblock is or whether it is true or not, if we believe it, the effects can be limiting.

We don't know the condition of the hearts of people who have hurt us, so we can't judge their actions. We don't have to spend our energy blaming others for their past behavior. It is absolutely critical, however, that we evaluate the impact of those actions on how we see the world.

We all want to be safe. We don't want to be in pain. But if we don't recognize that the hurt we are feeling may be from the past, we may not respond to the current situation as positively as we could. We might react to the pain of the past and miss a positive opportunity in the present.

That's a lesson I need to remember in my own interactions. I need to make sure that I communicate in a way that makes my intentions clear. I need to do all I can to provide a pain-free place to talk, even if the person I am trying to talk to is me. Just as important, on those days when I feel like I have been thrown out, I need to remember that not everyone is out to harm me. There might be a good soul looking out for me on a lonely road. There may be a friend or even a stranger who only wants to help me get the attention I need to heal my wounds.

Isolating ourselves to some degree seems to be the pattern of choice for those of us who have experienced the pain of betrayal. It doesn't matter much what form that betrayal took; it could have been a business partner, spouse, friend, coach, or parent who let us down. I can't begin to count the number of women and men who have come to my office seeking help to heal from the pain of broken trust.

One of the most common scenarios is typified by a young woman we will call Jenny. Jenny was struggling in her latest relationship. She described a wonderful young man to me and said she loved him very much. She told me about three other relationships she had been in over the last several years, each with a similarly fine young man for whom she cared greatly. Her description of the problem went something like this:

"There is something really wrong with me. I think maybe I'm crazy. I have been close to engagement with four men in the last few years. Every one of them was great, just what I wanted. But when the relationship became serious, I found a way to end it. There is nothing wrong with them. It must be me."

We met several times, and her concern grew. The man she was currently dating was going to ask her to marry him soon. She knew it was coming and was getting more terrified with each passing day. One day, she just broke down in my office and asked me in tears what she was supposed to say if he popped the question.

I asked, "What do you want to say?"

"I want to say yes, but I'm not sure I can. On the other hand, I don't want to hurt him. That is devastating. I know just how that feels, and it is horrible."

"How do you know how it feels?"

"I don't want to talk about it. I have moved on."

I asked the next question: "Will you please tell me what happened?"

Jenny wouldn't talk at first, but after some coaxing, she tearfully shared the experience of her first engagement. As a freshman, she had been engaged to a wonderful guy who she knew without a doubt was Mr. Right. He was everything she wanted. The week before the wedding, however, he called it off.

There was a long silence, and then Jenny continued. "The invitations were already sent. It was a humiliating time for me. I am glad we didn't marry. It turned out that he was not worthy for the temple and had been lying to me about that and a hundred other things."

After a brief pause so she could calm herself, I asked her if she thought it was crazy for her to be a little suspicious of potential husbands.

She burst into tears and went on. "You don't understand. I really thought this was the one. I didn't know he was lying. I felt like my prayers had been answered and I should marry him. I made that mistake once, and I don't want to make it again. I don't want to spend eternity with the wrong guy."

Jenny had no confidence in her ability to know who could be trusted, at least in the potential-husband category. She had decided that the only way to be sure she didn't make a mistake was to not get close enough to any man to have that decision to make.

Jenny needed to restore her confidence and learn how to trust herself about whom she could trust. I can report that with very little help, she did just that and married bachelor number four. It has been almost seven years, and they are doing very well and so are their kids.

When we take away all chances to fail, we automatically remove all opportunities for success. Just a little practical note here: It is impossible to remove all risk from any part of our earthly existence. Many times, the fear of doing something wrong keeps us from making any choice where the outcome seems in doubt. We must not let fear paralyze us. The question is, How can we rebuild our confidence and become dependable trusters? Well, as the New York cab driver replied when asked how one gets to Carnegie Hall, "Practice, practice, practice."

A Look at Boundaries

To understand the process of coming out from behind those self-protecting and inhibiting walls and learning to trust again, let's try looking at boundaries. Picture a beautiful, five-acre parcel of land. There is an impressive stone wall all the way around the property. On top of the wall is a big wrought-iron fence. In other words, picture a wonderful place that is protected all the way around. Nobody can get through that security. This is your property.

In one corner of the property is a great, big farmhouse with a wraparound porch. There is a four-car garage and a lovely circular driveway that leads from the gate right up to the front porch. The gate is wrought-iron that matches the fence—beautiful but very secure. The gate looks out onto a serene, tree-lined neighborhood street.

Inside the gate, just as you enter the grounds, there is an orchard on your right. A little closer to the house, the driveway brings you to a big vegetable garden. As you look around, you begin to take in the beauty of the place. There is a wonderful garden full of flowers, with a place to walk and benches to sit on and contemplate or read. At the far end of the property are a baseball diamond and an outdoor sports court. The rest of the property is an open, groomed field, perfect for playing a game of soccer or flying a kite.

You have fortified yourself inside this place. You are unreachable. It is perfectly acceptable for you to stand inside the front gate and talk to people as they go by. You might even hand them a flower and let them look beyond to the superb grounds. No matter what you choose to do, unless you open the gate, you are completely protected.

There is a problem with this ideal place, though: It is no fun unless it's shared. You can enjoy the flowers, sit and read, and walk in the garden, but even those things are better when shared. So how do you learn to share without any risk? The answer is, you can't. But you can consider a more useful question: How can you learn to share with as little risk as possible?

The first step may be the hardest. Here is what you do. Pick someone you have talked to before, open the gate a little bit, and invite the person to the orchard to thin apples, or to have a piece of fruit, or to sit in the shade for a minute. After a little while, you can walk the person to the gate, thank him or her, and lock up securely behind the person.

What this shows you is that some people who come in will leave when asked. There really are people who will go only where you invite them to go.

As the friendship develops, you might ask the person to come in and help plant a couple of rows of the garden. Over time, your new friend progresses from the orchard to the ball field to the vegetable garden to the flower garden. When you have become quite comfortable, you may say, "Why don't you come sit on the front porch and we'll have some lemonade." Then you might say, "I've got a cool book I'd like you to read," and you invite your friend into the library.

If someone has proven trustworthy in each of these locations, then you might even invite that person into the kitchen. The kitchen is where you and the people you love play games and eat food. It is where you are a family. Everybody in the kitchen has proven that he or she can be trusted. The kitchen is not lonely but a happy and joyful place.

Have you got this picture in your mind?

Now, consider this: The house and grounds represent our lives. Many people who have been hurt feel powerless. They believe that if they invite people inside the gate, there is no way to stop them from going wherever they want. That is a lie. We have the right to insist that someone leave if we feel unsafe. In a much less dramatic example, we can ask a person to leave when he or she does not respect our rules. In fact, we can ask a person to leave anytime we wish, for whatever reason we want.

I should emphasize that this is not a justification for abandoning our commitments or devaluing our covenants. It is our right to ask any person to leave—but we must consider our commitments as we are evaluating whether or not to do so. That is why it is so important to be as certain as we can that a person is trustworthy before we invite that person in to begin with.

The first step in trusting yourself is inviting someone to get to know you and having it go well. Then the hope starts. If one person is trustworthy, there may be others, and you might be able to figure out who they are.

Choosing the first person to invite in is the toughest. It may be a family member or an old missionary companion. You may choose a therapist or a church leader. The important thing is that you begin to interact. If you have believed in a rule that says that no one can be trusted, it only takes one person who proves trustworthy to change the rule.

The sharing of self is the beginning of all intimacy. The more we know about someone, the closer we are. When we share an experience with someone, we have more common ground for a relationship with that person. Whenever we allow anyone to know more about us, it naturally builds a broader foundation for understanding between us. Disclosing ourselves is the beginning step of trust. Such trust invites others to respond, and so we begin to move closer as that invitation is given and responded to.

Intimacy means being able to make more accurate relationship choices. The more we know about people, the better equipped we are to interact with them. The closer we become, the more clearly we see their needs and strengths. They are also better able to see us clearly and to interact effectively. The more we know about someone, the safer we can be.

That doesn't mean that we like what we know or that we are comfortable with that person. Sometimes the people we know the most about might not deserve our trust.

For example, the Lamanite generals had an intimate knowledge of Captain Lehi in the Book of Mormon. That knowledge played a big part in their plans for war.

"And now behold it came to pass, that when the Lamanites had found that Lehi commanded the city they were again disappointed, for they feared Lehi exceedingly; nevertheless their chief captains had sworn with an oath to attack the city; therefore, they brought up their armies" (Alma 49:17).

They had obviously met Captain Lehi before and knew what to expect. The point to emphasize here is that sometimes the people we know best are not safe for us.

This can pose a problem for us culturally. It is not easy to admit that a sister or uncle is toxic for us. We believe that if we are nice, we should love everybody. If we treat them nicely, they will behave nicely. That is not always true. We want it to be, but it just isn't.

When People Can't Be Trusted

For Latter-day Saints, this challenge goes even deeper. Our cultural or religious assumption is that people are basically good and we should trust them and be nice to them. Once they are in the gate, because they are nice, they should be able to go wherever they want. If we stop them, we're judging them harshly, or building walls. On the other hand, our own actual experience has likely taught us that not all people are nice—in fact, some people are evil. That is hard for many of us to accept.

Some of our difficulty may come from misunderstanding what we have been taught about judgment. In a fireside address given at Brigham Young University on March 1, 1998, Elder Dallin H. Oaks addressed wonderfully the issue of judging: "I have been puzzled that some scriptures command us not to judge and others instruct us that we should judge and even tell us how to do it. . . . I have become convinced that these seemingly contradictory directions are consistent when we view them with the perspective of eternity. The key is to understand that there are two kinds of judging: final judgments, which we are forbidden to make, and intermediate judgments, which we are directed to make, but upon righteous principles" ("'Judge Not' and Judging," *Ensign*, August 1999, 7).

We know that the world around us is not entirely good or entirely bad, so we must make the appropriate judgments that Elder Oaks suggests to help keep ourselves and those we love safe. We can extend trust based on our evaluations of people's trustworthiness, but we should also recognize that people can change and our evaluations may change over time.

We can choose not to invite someone in for a number of mundane but justifiable reasons. For example, "I don't have enough time" and "We have nothing in common" are perfectly acceptable reasons not to have everyone in. In order to qualify as good people, we don't need to treat everyone the same. That may sound silly, but many don't open up because they feel that in order to be fair, if they allow anyone in, they must allow everyone in. It's okay—in fact, it's very healthy—to have some orchard friends, some ball-field friends, and some front-porch friends.

Once people make it to the front porch, do they have to stay there forever? No. People aren't perfect. They can make a mistake and be sent back outside the gate at any time. They can also goof up and yet you can decide to let them stay. The main thing to remember is that *it's always your decision.*

Sometimes people worry that they are being self-righteous or ungrateful if they set boundaries that exclude certain friends or family members from the more intimate parts of their lives. We need to clarify that setting boundaries is about safety, not exclusion. We set boundaries not just for ourselves but for everyone in our lives. But learning to set boundaries can seem like we are limiting and judging others. Let me use the case of Debbie to illustrate.

Like many of my clients over the years, Debbie had experiences in her younger years that made trusting people very difficult. She had been sexually and physically abused as a girl by a man who was a distant relative and trusted family friend. Fear and shame had kept her from revealing this experience to anyone.

When we met, she had suffered a failed marriage and was contemplating dating again. She was a great mom, a woman of character and testimony. Her personality was kind and giving. I was interested to hear her say that her failed marriage and her fear of dating came from the same source. Debbie didn't trust anyone. She really believed that no one—in particular, no man—could be trusted. She felt that the only possibility for her to live a safe and secure life was to live alone.

Debbie's life experience was in direct conflict with the metaphor of the gate and house we used to describe the process of trust building. She believed that if she opened the gate, whoever entered could go wherever they wanted. That was not much of a stretch, given her experience. She walked her way through the empowering process of learning that she really could control how far people could go.

Things were moving right along when she came to another dilemma. It is one that I have heard repeated many times in different ways as people begin to set meaningful boundaries. Debbie's dilemma sounded like this: "My mom deserves to be in the kitchen even if she can't be trusted; after all, she is my mom."

Is this true? Does Debbie "owe" her mother, no matter what? Is she compelled to offer her most trusting place?

We need to clarify that boundaries are not about how we treat other people; they are about how much we trust them. The friends and acquaintances we meet at the gate or work with in the orchard should all be treated with civility and courtesy. This model is simply a vision for us personally. We don't hand out T-shirts or name cards saying, "Hi, I'm Bob. I'm just an orchard friend." We don't announce in the Sunday bulletin, "My mom can't be trusted, so the front porch is as far as she gets."

Mom can feel loved, safe, and secure no matter what level of trustworthiness she is capable of. She never even needs to know that she isn't in the kitchen. The boundaries are safety and management tools for us. They are invisible to everyone else.

It is also important to remember that the boundaries I have established for myself don't necessarily correspond with those of others. I know people who only have one boundary; the front gate is, in essence, labeled *in* or *out*. Some gates say, "Come on in and do whatever you want." Those are the gates where you can get a life history and intimate details of a person's life in the checkout line at the grocery store.

What did Debbie do? She trusted herself and came to understand that setting appropriate boundaries made it possible for her and her mother to have a relationship in which they were both safe and comfortable.

When we understand and are able to implement this power to choose who may come inside the gate, we are better prepared to protect ourselves from those who know our culture and prey upon it. They may be few in number, but they do a great deal of harm.

It is important to realize that those who intentionally wish to do us harm will often use any means to fool us. Those who know our culture well might even quote a scripture or two to justify their behavior. For example, every predator and perpetrator of evil I've ever known who is familiar with the Church can quote D&C 64:9–10 verbatim. I've had them do it to me or those I was counseling a thousand times. The scripture reads, "Wherefore, I say unto you, that ye ought to forgive one another; for he that forgiveth not his brother his trespasses standeth condemned before the Lord; for there remaineth in him the greater sin. I, the Lord, will forgive whom I will forgive, but of you it is required to forgive all men."

At first glance, it may seem as if the scripture is saying that no matter what you do to me, I have to forgive you. If I don't, I have done a worse thing than you did. That is not true. The very next verse says, "And ye ought to say in your hearts—let God judge between me and thee, and reward thee according to thy deeds" (D&C 64:11).

Simply stated, I should turn final judging over to God. I'm not going to pass final judgment on you. I will leave that to the Lord because that is His role. Note that it doesn't say the wrong-doer is not going to pay. Just as important, it doesn't say that I have to be with a person no matter what he or she does to me. This scripture frees the victim from necessity of continuing in an unsafe situation and the responsibility of passing final judgment.

What if some of the people you love most are toxic for you or harm you? Many times, they won't even know that what they are doing is hurtful or restrictive. You may be asking, "How can I love someone and not be able to be around that person?"

We can't change anyone but ourselves. No matter how much we love some people, if their behavior is not good for us, we must protect ourselves. Deciding not to spend time with someone whom you love or who loves you is hard. Even deciding to spend less time with an acquaintance can seem difficult.

Remember, however, that you have the right to choose to be in the best possible place you can. There is a great example in the Book of Mormon that illustrates this principle beautifully. In Ether 12, Moroni interjects his words into the translation of the Jaredite record. Here he gives counsel and reviews some of his dealings with the Lord. Moroni is clearly unaware that he will write more in the future. He takes this opportunity to bid farewell to the future readers of the Book of Mormon. In his farewell, he clearly expresses his love for the Lamanites. Here are his words from Ether 12:38: "And now I, Moroni, bid farewell unto the Gentiles, yea, and also unto my brethren whom I love, until we shall meet before the judgment-seat of Christ . . ."

By calling them "my brethren whom I love," Moroni shows us that he has reconciled with his old enemies. He is willing to express his love in a way that is a testimony of his commitment to the Savior.

Later, as he begins his own writings, he paints the picture of his love for the Lamanites. He prays that the Book of Mormon and his writings in particular may be of value to them in the future. Here is the account from Moroni 1:1–4:

> Now I, Moroni, after having made an end of abridging the account of the people of Jared, I had supposed not to have written more, but I have not as yet perished; and I make not myself known to the Lamanites lest they should destroy me.
>
> For behold, their wars are exceedingly fierce among themselves; and because of their hatred they put to death every Nephite that will not deny the Christ.
>
> And I, Moroni, will not deny the Christ; wherefore, I wander whithersoever I can for the safety of mine own life.
>
> Wherefore, I write a few more things, contrary to that which I had supposed; for I had supposed not to have written any more; but I write a few more things, that perhaps they may be of worth unto my brethren, the Lamanites, in some future day, according to the will of the Lord.

We learn several very important things from these excerpts from the prophet Moroni's writings:

He loves the Lamanites.

He is committed to sharing the word with them so that they might benefit from the gospel.

He cannot live with them or they will kill him.

Moroni knows that he must be alive to do what will eventually benefit those who would destroy him. Although he cares deeply for them, he cannot live with them. That is because of them, not him.

The same can be true for us. In the most extreme cases, if we don't separate ourselves from someone in our lives, we are in mortal danger. More often, however, the need to distance ourselves from those we love is about avoiding unnecessary hurt.

This distancing can take many forms. It can mean divorce or separation from a spouse. It could be that we need to relocate in order to get some distance from our parents, in-laws, or siblings. It may just mean spending less time with a suffocating friend. We give up one thing to protect something more valuable.

Many times, we feel guilty or selfish; we avoid making these decisions even when we know what is hurting us. It's easier to sacrifice ourselves than to take the chance of hurting or offending others. But by protecting ourselves, we may be preventing more serious future pain. Remember the words of Moroni: "wherefore, I wander whithersoever I can for the safety of mine own life" (Moroni 1:3).

Surviving in a Toxic Environment

One of the important steps in recovering from past injuries and becoming better trusters is to stop injecting poison into our systems. Abraham Lincoln has been quoted as saying, "If you want to drain a pond, the first order of business is to make sure no more water gets in." We need to make the choice to be actively engaged in keeping poison out of our lives.

Being aware that we can choose to avoid situations and people who are toxic to us is essential to our healing. This is how we keep toxic water from entering the pond of our minds. In the case of Moroni and the Lamanites, he avoided them completely. Because of the extreme nature of the threat they posed, he could not have any contact with them at all. Most of us don't have that level of threat in our lives.

When we discover a person or place that is toxic to us, we need to protect ourselves and those we love appropriately. However, we must also be aware that on occasion, we might choose to be in that toxic place. Doesn't it seem like the choice of whether or not to enter a dangerous place would be a simple one? It is not that simple. Here are some examples to illustrate how difficult that choice can be:

My sister is toxic for me, and she will be at

the family reunion.

the baptism.

the mission farewell.

the wedding.

That woman in the ward is insensitive and unkind, and she will be

in Relief Society.

in Sunday School.

at temple night.

As you can imagine, there are a number of things on those lists that I might want to be involved in. In the past, I might have just chosen to go to the event and endure the pain. Other times, I would just stay home and endure the pain of missing something I wanted to do. In either case, I would then spend countless hours in negative self-appraisal: "What is wrong with me? Why can't I get over this?"

If you're thinking there must be a more productive way to deal with this dilemma, take heart. There is. There are two analogies I have used over the years that seem to provide helpful coping strategies for avoiding this toxicity.

One is the concept of preparing to work in a toxic-waste facility. We can, with practice, be safe in almost any situation if we prepare effectively. Think of those TV or movie scenes in which scientists or medical professionals don hazmat suits to avoid deadly poison or infection. They move freely in the most toxic environments imaginable. They communicate and contribute without fear of contamination because the suits protect them by blocking all the dangerous stuff.

Every time we know we are going to be in a potentially toxic environment, we need to suit up. It takes a bit of preparation, but because we know what we are dealing with, we can block it. We can be assured that we can be in the environment in relative safety. We can do what we need or want to do without compromising our emotional health.

The second analogy is the idea of noise-canceling earphones. They are comfortable and can be programmed to block completely any harmful or destructive noise. Not only that, but they can be constructed in a way that will enhance the healing and pleasant sounds we encounter.

In both cases, remember that the toxicity protection is invisible. You have the suit or the earphones on, but nobody knows. Those people who are potentially damaging to you can't see them. There is no hurt to others—just protection for the user.

So how do you put the suit on or cover your ears with sound protection? How does it work?

As a therapist, my favorite example of a toxic environment is a family reunion. Here is what that environment might sound like:

Glad you could make it for once.

Maybe next year you will have a husband to drag along.

Looks like you've been eating well this past year.

You still driving that old Chevy?

Even if none of those comments would be a surprise to you, they could all still be hurtful. For some people, anticipating such an event can ruin the whole year leading up to it. But the guilt of avoiding the event can be just as devastating. Also, they would miss being with the people there whom they did love and want to see.

Even if what is being said or done follows a long-standing pattern of insensitivity or unkind behavior, you can refuse the poison. Here is how to suit up against toxic people and behavior. In your head, respond to each negative thought or feeling by using this phrase:

That's possible, or it could be . . .

Then insert what "it could be." Put an alternate, non-you-centered possibility in play. Here are some examples.

It could be . . .

you forgot your meds.

you saw your hair in the mirror and feel very, very bad about yourself.

you should seek professional help.

no one ever taught you to be kind; how sad for you.

you must be hurting inside to be so nasty.

The responses you have in your head to the potential poisonous comments can run from the humorous to the very serious. The thing to remember is that the phrase "it could be" is a very real, effective way of refusing to drink the poison. There really are a million reasons people react insensitively; we can't know for sure what they are in any individual circumstance. That is why trying to assign intent to others is so futile. The why here is not very important, even if we could know what it was. The important thing to remember in using toxic suits and filters is that how others choose to behave is about them, not you.

Let's use the story of my friend Rachel as an example. Rachel's mother was a great person in many ways. However, she had a weakness that caused Rachel great pain for many years. Rachel's mom was not nurturing. She was just not very tender.

She was a hard worker and a very fair-minded person. She had a testimony of service and served with a consistency that was admirable. She recognized the good in others but failed to appreciate her own.

She never said "I love you" to Rachel or her siblings and was not very complimentary. My friend wanted to hear how proud her mother was of her. She wanted to have her mom ask how she was feeling. She wanted to know for sure that her mom was interested in what the grandkids were up to.

After realizing that her mom was just too unaware of or unable to share her feelings, we decided that Rachel needed to find a way to eliminate the toxic thoughts she was having. So we decided to try "or it could be . . ."

When her mom would seem too cold or distant and the thought came into Rachel's mind that she wasn't very lovable, Rachel would override that thought with "Or it could be that this good, sweet mother of mine would love to nurture but she just can't. It could be that Mom is too tender to even go there." This changed "Something is wrong with me" into "My mom is a great woman but not perfect." No big surprise there, because no person is perfect.

Not long after her mother's passing, Rachel read in her mom's journal the sweet and tender words she had always longed to hear. Her mother had been having those feelings all along. She was just unable, for whatever reason, to verbalize them.

By using that simple "or it could be . . ." technique, Rachel had been able to appreciate her mother and not let her mom's blind spot or weakness in one area keep them apart.

Steps Toward Trusting

Once we gain the confidence to trust our evaluative skills when it comes to people, we are free to interact with others without as much fear. This skill will help us get over the hard lessons of the past that taught us not to trust in the first place.

How do we become better at trusting? What can we do? The steps I find most effective are really questions. There are three very simple ones. I have shared them hundreds of times with clients, and they work. If a person meets the standard set by these three questions, then letting that person in is worth a try. But remember, just inside the gate—this is not a free pass to go wherever he or she wishes. The more consistency you see over time, the more reliable your evaluations will become. Look for a pattern of the following.

Let's say you've met a woman you are considering opening the gate to as a friend. Ask yourself these questions:

1. Do her actions and words match? Is what she says in harmony with what she does? Do her actions and words seem to come naturally, as if she is truly being herself? Is how she talks about others in harmony with how she treats them?

2. Is what she's doing or saying credible? Is her portrayal of herself and others reasonable? Are her comments and compliments believable?

3. How does it feel to me when she is around?

This last question may be the most important one of all. Many people have dismissed their ability to hear the promptings of the Spirit. This exercise will reconnect you with that still, small voice of warning or encouragement.

Remember, take small steps at first. Have faith in this simple system, and take your time. Observe as long as you need to in order to be able to answer the questions. There is no need to be in a rush. As you get better at asking and answering these questions in your mind, it will become second nature to you.

Here are some possible scenarios to practice. If someone appears to be completely credible and says reasonable things but it doesn't feel right, don't invite that person further into your life until it does feel right. Have the confidence to know that the choice is yours. You choose how and where to set the boundaries, and only you can change them.

For example, what if you really love this person but you feel like something is just not right? Err on the side of the Spirit. I can't tell you how many times in marriage counseling I've had a man or woman (usually a woman) say to me, "I knew something was wrong before I ever married this person." I've had people say, "I knew it was not quite right, but we had already sent out the invitations, and it was too embarrassing not to get married." I promise that it is better to be embarrassed about not getting married than to have a horrible marriage and an ugly divorce. Again, the key thing to remember is that you set the boundaries and you get to choose. No person or circumstance should compel or rush you to do something that feels wrong to you.

Learning to trust yourself is a key to making other decisions as well. For example, consider the question of where to attend school or what to choose as a major area of study. Input from those we love is often helpful. Research is a must, of course. But in the end, it comes back to trusting what you observe and how you feel. The choice is, after all, yours.

Most often, the experiences you have with this process will be positive rather than negative. When you decide to invite new people into your life or let them come closer, whenever they prove to be trustworthy, your confidence jumps up a step or two. It's like anything else—if you do it well a few times, your skill and your confidence increase.

I love the perspective that Elder Neal A. Maxwell of the Quorum of the Twelve gives to the process: "It is better to trust and be sometimes disappointed than to be forever mistrusting and be right occasionally" ("Insights from My Life," BYU devotional address, October 26, 1976).

I am not suggesting that we put on rose-colored glasses and pretend that the world is completely safe and perfect. We need to be aware of the negative because that awareness helps protect us. However, we must dwell on the positive because that is a choice that improves our lives and the lives of those around us.

Much of life is about how we choose to see it. One of my favorite stories about perspective is the story of Roy Gappmier. Roy was a patriarch who lived in our ward when I was a young married student at Brigham Young University. We lived in a family ward, and Roy seemed ancient to us. Every day, he worked in his yard, steadying himself with a crutch because his hips and knees were kind of feeble and he was barely able to get around. He grew the most beautiful flowers imaginable and loved sharing them with people passing by.

The road in front of Roy's house was torn up because they were putting in a new, wider street with sidewalks on both sides. It was the talk of the neighborhood. Everyone had complained; in fact, one man had stood up in priesthood meeting and shaken his fist at the entire congregation and told them to slow down because their reckless driving up and down the road was getting dust on his cherries and would make his market price less, and it didn't have to be that way if everyone would just slow down and do the right thing. Feelings ran pretty high.

Passing by one day, we saw Roy out in his yard. I was young and foolish and sort of got on the bandwagon. I said to Roy that it was just horrible that they were going to widen this road, and it was such a mess, and it looked to me as if, based on the way they had it staked out, they were going to take out some of his flower beds. In fact, it looked like they were going to tear out the big oak tree on the corner. His eyes teared up, and I thought, *Oh my gosh, what have I done here?*

He said, "My wife and I" (his wife had passed away not too many years before and was basically the love of his life) "planted that tree when we first moved in here almost seventy years ago. My kids played in it. They built tree houses in it."

The more he spoke, the more my heart ached for my having brought up the subject. And yet I found myself thinking, *Even Brother Gappmier, even the patriarch, even the man who looks for the good in everyone, can see that this road project is just foolishness and isn't being done well.* I began to review in my mind all the comments I'd heard from various sources.

Brother Gappmier paused for just a second and said, "Yeah, it's going to be horrible to lose this old tree and these beautiful flowers, but in fact, there is only one thing I can think of that would be more beautiful than that tree." He smiled. "That's the thought of all the little children who live in the apartments playing safely up and down the road in front of the house here instead of the chance that we take when we have no sidewalks, which might lead these young people into danger."

And that was one of the first times in my life that I realized how important attitude was in all aspects of our lives—not just the complicated things, but the simple things as well. Brother Gappmier taught me a wonderful lesson: Even if you are emotionally engaged, if you look far enough and hard enough to get a real perspective on what is happening, you can usually find the good in a situation. And many times by looking, you find the right good, the best good—you find not only the goodness in things but the goodness in people. That's something for which I will ever be grateful to Roy Gappmier That day, he gave me something far more valuable than a flower as I passed his house; he gave me the insight and perspective required to understand the role I play in my own life. I'm the only one who can decide how I see the world.

Section 3

Abandoning the Scorekeeping Habit

Heavenly Father has given us the gift of agency to allow us to bless our lives and the lives of others. Setting appropriate boundaries and learning to trust others and ourselves will give us the calm assurance of safety. That confidence and safety enable us to feel the peace of God's love. If we don't feel that confidence, safety, and love, it might be because we are measuring ourselves by the world's standard rather than God's. Applying earthly standards of measurement to ourselves and others can be devastating. After all, we know who authored the standards of measurement for worldly success and power. The adversary wants us to measure our success by his standards.

For the purposes of our discussion here, we're going to give a name to this habit that so many of us have of measuring our lives according to standards that are in direct contrast to God's standard. We will call this practice scorekeeping. Scorekeeping, then, is the practice of measuring our relationship to others, ourselves, and God by the imperfect and insecure judgments of the world. By recognizing the impact of scorekeeping in our lives, and learning to set it aside, we can improve our relationships and diminish regrets.

Quiz: Are You a Scorekeeper?

Want to know if you are a scorekeeper? Here is a little quiz that will give you a better picture of the scorekeeping process and where you fit in it.

1. If you get help, do you feel indebted (not just grateful but in debt)?

2. Is asking for help bad because it feels needy?

3. Is *needy* a very bad word?

4. Is it easier to give than receive?

5. Is there a lot of competition in your family of origin?

6. Do you feel obligated to call your mom once a week?

7. Is *lazy* a very bad word?

8. Do you owe anyone a call or letter?

9. Do you feel diminished in some way by another person's accomplishment?

10. If something good happens to someone, do you feel a little resentment?

11. Do you compare yourself to others and feel the need to know somehow if you are ahead or behind?

12. Do you compare yourself to others to feel justified in what you are doing?

13. If your spouse buys a new gadget, do you feel you should get something new, too?

14. At the last church potluck, did you know whose funeral potatoes were the best?

15. If your husband goes somewhere with the guys, do you bring it up the next time you want to go somewhere with your friends to justify your time away?

Many yes answers to those questions might signal that you are a scorekeeper. Don't be alarmed; most of us are, to some extent. There are lots of reasons we might feel the need to keep score.

One reason would be to feel like we could control the actions of somebody else by obligating them through our behavior; for example: "If I cook his favorite meal, he will have to go to church on Sunday." Trying to compel someone to do something we want is a prime reason for keeping score.

Another common motivation for scorekeeping is to create guilt in someone else or relieve guilt that we are feeling. Most of the time, this is not very effective because the scorekeeper doesn't make clear what is expected from the other person involved.

In order to get a rest from all the effects of keeping score, we need to find out how to dump the habit. That's all it is: an unneeded habit. Breaking the scorekeeping habit can prevent more emotional fatigue and pain than almost anything.

How Scorekeeping Happens

Keeping score is a habit that affects every area of our lives. It is so second nature that we might not even know we are doing it. And yet, it can be extremely taxing. It is like keeping spreadsheets on everything.

Scorekeeping is part of the adversary's plan. He tries to keep us tied to the material world by encouraging us to keep score in everything. The purpose of keeping score is not to assess our performance but to determine our place relative to those around us so that we can know if we are winning or losing. We have thousands of interactions with the people in our lives every day. A scorekeeper tries to keep track of every one in order to decide where he or she stands.

Here are two simple examples of what scorekeeping might look like.

Picture a husband playing golf on a Saturday afternoon and a wife at home with the children doing chores. The wife decides what this golf game is worth and how she will collect the bill. She may decide that a round of golf for her husband justifies a new pair of shoes for her.

Picture a husband working hard at his job. The husband

decides that the wife is at home every day living a life of leisure because he works so hard. He decides what that leisure costs and how he could collect the bill. He may decide that working hard at work means he doesn't have to do any chores at home.

In both cases, the partner being scored has no idea it is happening. The spouse doing the scoring is making assumptions and placing arbitrary values on whatever is going on—adding or subtracting points to an action or event.

Keeping score requires assigning a value to every interaction. In order to decide who owes whom in this system, a scorekeeper must evaluate the point value both negatively and positively for every interaction, both real and imagined. To track the score, I must decide every person's motive for every one of life's exchanges. This evaluation has to include the condition of the other person's heart and his or her intent. Good people keep score very differently from the way selfish or arrogant people do it.

Hence, if I don't want to get cheated, I have to do the scoring. I must make these evaluations by myself. I don't include anyone to help me decide what everything is worth. So I need to evaluate every action and interaction with the question, Who meant to do what? I have to give the action a value and evaluate the motivation in order to assign an overall value.

Let's look at an example with me as the scorekeeper. If I wash the dishes, that would be worth 1,000 points. Dishwashing is generally not on my chore chart. But if the designated dishwasher does it, it isn't worth nearly as much because he was just doing his job. It's the same activity, but when I so selflessly do the dishes, it is about love and sacrifice, so it gets me more points. Even though this example is given some-what tongue in cheek, it is easy to see how the process might work in my mind. This process requires almost instantaneous and constant evaluation and comparison.

That kind of immediate comparative scorekeeping has failure built in for any relationship—that is why Satan loves it. Successful relationships are about balance over time. Sometimes I'm ahead; sometimes my boss is. Sometimes my spouse is ahead; sometimes it's me. Taking the time to have some confidence in the give-and-take of a healthy relationship requires commitment. Satan hates commitment. It requires mutual concern, which is charity. You know how he feels about charity. Perhaps most important, it requires trust. Commitment and charity require us to trust our judgment. When we have confidence in our ability to choose wisely, we become better and more dependable partners in any endeavor.

If I am scorekeeping, when can I be happy and rest? Never, because I'm just too busy keeping track of seemingly endless complex columns of point totals.

How many times do I hear husbands say, "I am always in trouble"? And how many wives say, "He never asks me what I think"? That's about scorekeeping. When we're busy assuming and making assessments and calculations, we don't take the time to talk. We are caught up in the process of keeping track rather than simply loving and growing. We are less inclined to solve and learn and more inclined to experience blame and regret with both ourselves and others.

Not only is this process most often fruitless; it is exhausting. For example, is a night out with the boys or a night at book club the same thing? Or, is spending $50 to go play a round of golf equivalent to going to the movies and only spending $15? Even though the activities take roughly the same amount of time, do they have the same value? Are we measuring fun or time? If I make him go to the family reunion, I ask myself, "What is this going to cost me?" And in friendships, keeping score could sound like, "She is always doing stuff for me; I had better find a way to pay her back." Do we rate by eternal implications? How many golf games does going to the temple get me? Our score-keeping ledger continues to grow in confusion and arbitrariness. No wonder we are so worn out.

Scorekeeping creates a false economy. If I think I know what something is worth, then I can try to manipulate your behavior with my product. If I am really, really nice to you, you have to let me go play ball on Thursday night . . . and I'll decide when I've been nice enough. If you don't let me go play ball, I'll be disappointed because I've been nice to you all week. In my mind, they are connected. I'm making a purchase. Being nice should equal playing ball.

When I begin to assign value to things, I can't overlook motive. Actions are driven by motive, so intent must be estab-lished if I am to keep score effectively. The condition of the heart matters. If my friend intended to hurt me, the number of negative points I assess to her actions is higher than if she were just insensitive or not very aware. I must make an evaluation of every person's intent in order to keep track of where I stand.

Scorekeeping sums are never clear-cut. I get to decide what the other person is thinking. Rather than saying to myself, "He doesn't get it" or "He made a mistake," I might assume, "He knew he was hurting me, and he did it anyway. That's mean." So he gets more negative points. I don't ask. I don't check in. I just put it in the ledger as I am inclined to interpret it. That's a real problem. Maybe he's completely unaware of the hurt. I might be devastated, and so it goes in the big devastation column of my scorekeeping ledger, but he doesn't even know how far behind he is or why.

Our evaluations are also based on our emotional scales. So even if we wanted to make comparable and fair assessments of what someone else was feeling, the difference in how we feel makes that even more complex. On a scale of one to ten, one being of no importance to me emotionally and ten being of great emotional impact, I personally don't have any tens unless somebody dies. I don't even have many sixes or sevens. My wife has lots of nines on her scale. In fact, anything having to do with our grandchildren is a 9.5.

Scorekeeping: A Competitive Sport

Keeping score is all about comparisons and turns life into an "-er thing."

Who is prettier?

Who is smarter?

Who is better?

Who is richer?

Endless mutually exclusive comparisons take place. If I am, you can't be; if you are, then I am not.

In order to get a leg up, I can build myself up or tear you down. Both of those things happen a lot in the scorekeeper's world. In order to stay ahead, I can do something to put myself ahead compared to you, or I can do something to you in order to keep myself from feeling behind.

Most scorekeepers are just doing what they have been taught. We learn the economics of scorekeeping in our families of origin, from our parents, siblings, extended family members, and those close to us. These people don't generally set out to do harm, but harm is the natural result of scorekeeping.

Do any of these examples sound familiar?

"That is just the way Dad is. He is your father, no matter how bad his temper gets."

"I don't really want to go to this dinner, but what would the other women in the Relief Society think if I weren't there?"

"We will get out of there as soon as we can, but Grandma would be mad if we didn't come."

"You might think you want to be an engineer, but if you didn't follow in the family business, it would break our hearts. We did all of this for you."

"Go ahead and go—don't think about me here alone."

Throughout our lives, among families and friends and even in the workplace, keeping score can manifest itself through controlling or defining pronouncements designed to keep us in our place. These rules act as either constant point subtracters or point adders. Examples may be:

"You have legs like Sharron."

"You might not know it, Molly, but it's only a matter of time until the other people around here realize how really weak your skills are."

"You are mom's twin sister."

"I'll give you this—compared to your usual reports, it's pretty good."

"You get everything without working because you're the baby."

"If you don't agree with me, then you don't love me."

"David likes me best; he just won't tell you."

Scorekeeping is a way to try to control people. I might have been taught in my family, for example, that if I perform a specific task or set of tasks for you, you are obligated to do some specific task for me. If I do this, this, and this, you've got to do this, this, and this. When tradition or misguided teaching allows us to bind a member of our family to a specific action, we can control them. And unless we make a conscious choice not to play our family game, we can be controlled ourselves. Here are some examples. Be aware that these things are generally not spoken out loud; they are just assumed.

"If I take your side in an argument, then next time there is a family fight, you must be my ally."

"If I call you, then you have to call me, or I am justified in feeling unloved."

"If I go in the bedroom at a family gathering, you have to come and talk to me and see what's wrong. If you don't, you're a bad sister."

"When I call to share my problems and you don't listen to me attentively and take my side, you are also the enemy by siding with them."

"You must downplay your achievements and overcompliment me for mine or you are arrogant and self-aggrandizing."

This whole process of scorekeeping presupposes that life is a zero-sum equation. That is, everything that someone else gets diminishes me or what I can have in some way. If there is only so much of anything, then whatever you have lessens my chance of getting it.

Why can't we all be the smart one?

Is there only so much success and intelligence?

Does the same apply to joy or kindness or love?

None of these attributes or skills are exclusive—except in the minds of scorekeepers.

The Lasting Effects of Scorekeeping

If a scorekeeper is really good, he or she can score a hit that will take points away from another forever. At least that is how it may seem.

An example of this can be seen in the life of a girl named Kelly. In her case, the lasting hit was something her sister said to her when she was a Beehive. Picture a twelve-year-old new to the Young Women program. Imagine how she looked up to the older girls, her sister in particular.

Kelly had worked hard on a particular project. When she got a little recognition for that during Young Women opening exercises one day, her sister had to get some points. Instead of celebrating with her younger sister, she made a joke of the moment. She said to her friends, just loudly enough for her little sister to hear, "She had the choice of cute or churchy, and we can see what she chose."

I don't know what the intent of the older sister was or if she even realized what she was doing. I do know the impact of that statement on that tender little Beehive. Many years later, in my office, Kelly and I talked about it.

Kelly was an active member of the Church and had married a great young man. They had two beautiful little girls.

Kelly's problem was that she didn't feel happy about herself or her life. She said she wasn't depressed—just sad. I agreed that she didn't seem depressed, but privately, I thought that she seemed more angry than sad. She had a lot of passion and energy, which would typically be absent in a depressed person. Kelly said that the hardest thing for her to do was go to church. She had no idea why, since she had always loved church and had possessed a strong testimony for as long as she could remember. But it seemed like over the years, she had begun to feel "churchy" and self-righteous whenever she was at church. After all, who did she think she was?

After a few conversations, we discovered another interesting and pertinent feeling. No matter how hard she worked at it, Kelly never felt attractive. She was a very pretty young woman, so something was clearly out of whack here.

I asked her if she felt like she was competing with the women around her. She laughed and said, "If you had been raised in my family, you would know we are in competition with everybody."

We began to untangle the knot from that moment on. We learned about scorekeeping. We talked about being hurt. She put two and two together and connected how she felt to her sister's comments. There was no repressed memory here; she had always remembered the embarrassment of that day and others. She just had not connected those hurtful comments to how she felt now. When she finally did, it was cathartic. She discovered that she had unknowingly been keeping score and always felt behind.

I can report that now Kelly goes to church and loves the gospel happily and even feels pretty. Her choice to rid herself of the scorekeeping habit eliminated an imaginary requirement for her happiness and positive self-worth.

The Savior described one of the reasons He came to earth: "I am come that they might have life, and that they might have it more abundantly" (John 10:10). He didn't say that only a few would get to enjoy a full abundance.

As God's children, we are in a precious position. Unlike earthly kings, all of God's children are heirs to the throne. The abundant rule in God's family is "the more the merrier," literally. Since that is the case, why do we insist on keeping score?

That's Not Fair!

The "it has to be fair" life philosophy is a prime directive for scorekeepers. This seems okay at first glance, but of course this assumption requires someone to decide the value of everything in order to assure fairness. "Determining fairness" is scorekeeping. If I am always the one who gets to say what is fair, I can easily stay on top.

Sometimes we set up in our children an expectation for fairness; in fact, we often go out of our way to make everything with our kids fair. In the process, we sometimes confuse "fair" with "equal" or "without limits." My brother is older than me, so he was legally eligible to drive before I was. That is fair but not equal. However, I remember saying to my mom, "It's not fair. Craig gets to do everything." My guess is that Craig might have been saying something like this at about the same time: "Mom, it isn't fair. I have to go to work this summer, and all Kim has to do is play ball with his friends."

We grew up believing that if Johnny gets something, I should get the same thing or something equivalent. This thinking can create a sense of entitlement. In order for it to be fair, I must have what someone else has.

"I should get a new car when I turn sixteen because that is what all the kids at my school get."

"I am a Johnson; we always get what we want."

"My dad practically built this town—I should run it."

We even disguise the subtler form of "scorekeeping to obligate" by claiming that it would only be fair if others would respond like we want them to. We teach this contradictory principle all the time to children. For example, "If you're good, I'll give you an ice-cream cone." So they just extend that to say, "If I want something, here's what I have to do." This isn't about fairness at all. It is about indebtedness. We do it all the time without even realizing how we are confusing the idea of fairness.

"If I give the kids dancing lessons, they'll be happy with me."

"If I make cookies, he will have to clean his room."

"If I go to his stupid party, then he must come to mine."

"If I provide lessons and camps, the kids will utilize their talents and be ever grateful."

Over a period of time, our children begin to feel like they get to decide what is fair and what isn't fair. "Well, it's not fair Mom. All the other kids who drive in high school have a car." "It's not fair. He made the team, and I didn't." We rarely hear, "He is a better player than I am" or "I understand that we can't afford another car."

It's Not My Fault

It is easy to see why scorekeepers never want to be behind. Being behind doesn't feel good. Scorekeepers who find themselves behind in the standings will look for ways to say, "It's not my fault." In order to do this well, scorekeepers can use "if only" statements. These statements keep blame or failure and the accompanying loss of points in the "it's not my fault" category. Here are some of my all-time favorites:

"If my parents had given me voice lessons, I would have been way better than Josh Groban."

"If I had his connections, I'd be rich, too."

"The only reason I didn't play is because the coach hates me."

"My sister spoiled it for me by being Little Miss Perfect."

"The other cheerleaders were jealous."

If blaming doesn't work, there is always the "it's not fair" category.

"Her parents knew the judges, so I was beaten before I started."

"The only reason he got in was because he is a minority."

"The only reason I didn't get in was because I'm a minority."

Many of these comments are more whines than excuses, really, but they are nevertheless very good tools to keep a person from losing points. If somehow you have been afflicted by some malevolent external force, you don't lose points. After all, it's not your fault.

Every day, we say or hear things like, "He thinks I'm . . ." or "She thinks that . . ." or "You only did that because . . ." That is what we use to give ourselves value. That is how we get the numbers to keep score. It feels like we have to jump through all the right hoops and check off all the right boxes in order to be loved.

Let me share a few possible examples. Sister Jones has a really great husband, and her kids play the violin. Her house is immaculate, and she always looks put together. Sister Smith's house is a mess, and she is still in her pajamas at noon. *What a loser I am,* Sister Smith thinks. *I will never catch up.*

On the other hand, maybe Sister Jones is thinking about Sister Smith, *She is a good, righteous woman. People really like her.* Of herself, she thinks, *Nobody comes to see me; they must not like me.* So Sister Jones is keeping score, and so is Sister Smith.

Scorekeeping is a cumulative process. We always want more points. Having fewer points means failure, since points are a reflection of how we feel about ourselves. The more points we have, the better we perceive ourselves to be.

Sometimes a score discrepancy seems so big that it just can't be overcome. Here is one of the best illustrations in my experience. I met with a couple whom we will call Bob and Mary. They had several children. Bob was a returned missionary; he had been a bishop and a seminary teacher. He was committed to his kids and wife. They had been married for more than twenty years. I asked if I could meet with them separately in order to get a sense of what each was feeling without the other one present.

I spoke first with Mary. I will never forget her first words of explanation for her visit: "It all started more than twenty years ago." Stop. When something is unresolved for more than twenty years by two people living together, that's a bad thing. But I can't tell you how many times it happens. When the poison of not forgiving goes on long enough, people just come to accept it. In cases like these, it is easy to see why we have been counseled by God not to hold on to grudges. The destructive effect on a person who won't let go—who chooses to be a victim by not forgiving and moving on—is devastating.

Mary told me her story. Never in their whole marriage had her husband been sensitive to her needs or placed her first. "My dad told me this was all wrong from the beginning. I should have listened."

Bob and Mary had dated for several months before getting married in the temple. "That was a wonderful time," she said. She had attended all of his church basketball games. They had a great team. He was the captain and point guard.

When Bob and Mary had been home from their honeymoon a few days, the multiregional playoffs started. This was a Friday evening and Saturday event. It would last all day Saturday if the team kept winning.

Mary was aware that the tournament was coming. After work on Friday, Bob happily put on his uniform and sweats.

Mary wasn't getting ready to go, so Bob asked her why. Her answer: "Now that you are married, you have more important things to do than playing ball."

He told her his team was depending on him. He hadn't seen his old roommates since the wedding.

Then she said (as she reported and he later confirmed), "Oh, you go ahead. I just don't feel like it."

It was in that moment that he dug a hole he still isn't out of. He chose a church ball game instead of his family. I am not here to judge the virtue of church ball or whether Bob was insensitive. I am simply pointing out why there was so much dissatisfaction and trouble in what appeared to be a pretty workable marriage.

Here are the things I found most troubling: Mary told him to go; she just didn't feel like going. He wasn't aware that she was not sharing what she really felt. He took what she said at face value. And once he discovered his mistake, it was too late— he was never getting out of that hole.

When we spoke, Bob had a much different story. He always felt in trouble. There had been some good mixed in, but for the most part, he felt like his life was a trudge from work to home to bed. Throw in the kids' sports and church, and that was his life.

I wish I could give you a happy ending. The marriage crumbled. Mary was never able to let go of Bob's decision to play ball. Bob is remarried and doing well. Mary has remarried, too; I hope it's going well for her.

Blame is not a very effective problem-solving tool, but it is vital to the scorekeeper. One of the biggest reasons for scorekeepers to assign blame instead of dealing with painful issues is the fear that if they deal with the issues, the final score might put them behind.

As with Bob and Mary, though, the real devastation of never resolving this kind of blaming is that the score becomes so lopsided over time that there is no way to reconnect. The fear of being behind is compounded over time. Without honest, blameless self-evaluation, we lose the ability to heal the wounds in our relationships.

We are imperfect beings in an imperfect world. The complexities of our existence make perfection impossible. That is one of the many reasons why our Father in Heaven warns against judging. His commandment refers not only to judging others but judging ourselves. Being too self-critical can be devastating. It is important to evaluate our lives every day in order to learn and grow. But we need to remember as we evaluate ourselves and others that our perfection is a process. We are on the way, not at the final destination.

Some of the wisest people I know go out of their way to avoid the trap of judgment, knowing the potential hurt it brings. Let me share a story of one of them that inspired me.

A close friend of mine, we'll call him Steve, was up for a huge promotion at work. It was a prestigious and highly sought-after position. Steve felt that he was qualified. In his mind, he had been assured that he was the front-runner. The decision was to be made by a search committee. He knew every person on that team and had worked with most of them.

When the decision was announced, they had chosen another person for the job. Steve was crushed. He asked for a few days of personal leave and just paused to get his life back in order. During his time off, two of his closest friends called on him to try to lessen his pain at being overlooked. In an effort to calm him, both reviewed in detail how and why the decision was made. There was a very real problem, though. Based on what they had shared with Steve, it was evident that one of them was lying. He was crushed again that one of his dear friends would lie to him. He started down the judgment trail. Perhaps Bob was not a friend at all and just wanted his real pal to get the job. Maybe Kent was jealous of Steve and just wanted to stick it to him.

Then Steve stopped. These were good men, tried and true. Could they maybe have just seen the situation differently? Was it possible that each was trying to protect him from hurt by leaving out something or embellishing something else? What would he gain by guessing or engaging in a witch hunt to find out for sure who had lied?

Did he need to be hurt more? Did he need to hurt others? He told me that he took a prayerful moment and came to peace. "Is that all?" I asked. "How did you resolve who the traitor was?"

He said, "It was easy. I just believed them both."

The Scorekeeping Double Standard

One of the most devastating types of scorekeeping is the habit of over-accepting blame. In this scenario, the scorekeeper is harder on himself or herself than on anyone else. This perspective particularly affects the scorekeeping of good people. These people hold themselves to a far higher standard than they hold others. What does it look like?

Your relationship with your children is likely a very good example of this double standard in action. Consider the conversations you have with yourself inside your head. Think about what feedback you give yourself. Then apply this test: If you saw a mother treating her daughter the way you treat yourself, what kind of a mom would you think she was? My guess is that *patient* and *loving* are not the words that leap to mind.

You can be benevolent with your daughter. That is not necessarily because she deserves it; part of that kindness is because you love her and know what a daughter needs. Well, you are a daughter, or a son—shouldn't you get scored in a more loving way? This kind of scorekeeping really points out how arbitrary our systems can be.

If your evaluation of your performance is completely negative when you compare it to how you would evaluate your child in the same situation, you are a self-defeating scorekeeper. That is especially hazardous when you partner up somehow with a person who feels entitled. When entitlement meets self-defeat, one partner can spend his or her whole life giving and giving in a relationship. At the same time, the other partner will happily spend life taking and taking and still think that it is not enough.

Examples of this inappropriate scorekeeping are everywhere. I know men who claim to have no idea why they were fired and yet they know full well in their hearts that they haven't done anything with their jobs for years. I know other people who work themselves to death and have never been appreciated. Neither one of those things is okay. And they are both a direct result of inappropriate scorekeeping.

Scorekeeping and Love

Scorekeeping can be particularly destructive when love is involved. We all want to be loved. But when scorekeeping enters the equation, problems arise, since love is thought of as something that has to be earned. The reality is that love is never purchased; it is always a gift.

It is difficult, if you are in the habit of feeling that love must be earned, to believe that someone would love you by choice. What if their love only appears to be a gift but really they are giving it to get something in return? What if their motivation for giving you love is just because it creates good endorphins for them? Is that a purchase? If the intended outcome of a person's sharing love is his or her own gain at someone else's expense, I think that is a purchase—and therefore, by definition, not truly love. Remember: Love is never purchased; it is always a gift. We must learn to give it as a gift and receive it as a gift—and learn to trust ourselves.

What if I'm motivated of my own free will and choice to love you? Do you owe me something for that? I have never before or since wanted anything in my life as much I wanted my wife, Lois, to love me. Anyone who knows us well will attest in court under any oath you choose that they have no idea how I managed to get her to marry me. If I wanted her to love me that much, doesn't it make sense that I would be nice to her? In fact, I did everything in my power so that she would fall in love with me. Was that a purchase? No, she chose me. She was not forced. Natural consequence is not the same as owing the bill. She chose me, and that makes her gift of love priceless.

Just a note here: Loving me is still her choice. For the record, I still try to do things to invite her to love me every day.

The interesting thing about giving love freely, without feeling forced or compelled, is that we intuitively know we are going to feel good about giving the gift *no matter how the other person responds.* That too is a gift. The best part of trusting in being able to feel genuine love is that when you give it and it is well received, you get to feel good twice.

Who decides what any act of love is worth in a relationship? It's unimportant, unless you're keeping score. If what I do is a positive thing and I do it of my own free will and choice, that's the reward. It is a gift, ergo it qualifies as love.

It is interesting that in marriage ceremonies, we often hear words like "give yourself to this person of your own free will and choice." Love is a gift; it can only be given by you. Love can't be compelled. Even God won't compel you to give it without your consent.

Some of us were taught that every act is self-serving:

"There is always an angle."

"There ain't no free lunch."

"You scratch my back, and I'll scratch yours."

Some suggest that God keeps score. I hope not. If he does, I'm in big trouble. I'm counting on the mercy of the Atonement, not justice. I believe firmly that God loves us, and not because we are particularly loveable. He loves us because He is our Father, and as our Father, He has chosen to love us.

Love and real concern for each of us is one of the miracles that separate God from Satan. Because of that love, we can be assured that when we deal with God, it's always about us. When we deal with the adversary, it's always about him.

If I have agency, I can give without need or expectation, can't I? I can also receive with great dignity. Frankly, for most of us, the problem isn't that we don't give well; it's that we don't receive well. It can seem like everything's suspect.

If we were taught that love has to be purchased, it follows that we must need to produce some kind of product in order to earn it. Yet our own experience should teach us that a purchase is not required. I have asked the following question to mothers hundreds of times, and I always get the same two answers. Here is the question: "How long did it take to love your child after she was born?" Here are the answers: "I loved her immediately" or "I loved her before she was born."

"When your child was born, you loved her immediately?"

"Yes."

"What product could she have produced to earn that affection?"

"None."

"So, the prerequisite for love is not a product or production of any kind. Is that right?"

"Yes."

I have often used this exercise to help married people understand that intimacy, and especially physical intimacy, is not a purchase. Too many couples have a hard time here. When intimacy becomes a power struggle instead of a source of power to build our marriages, we lose a great deal indeed.

Intimacy doesn't have to be about scorekeeping or earning. It should always be a gift.

Here is an example of how intimacy could look if there were no keeping score. Suppose that we were married, you and I, in the temple. We've been married a couple of years and don't have any kids. We have treated each other kindly. I know this has been a very hard week for you. You have a very important deliverable at work. Perhaps the project is a report or a presentation to a large group. It is a big deal, and you have worked hard on it. You call on the way home because you are running late and you don't want me to worry. You come in the door at 6:30 p.m., and I'm making you dinner. There are flowers on the table. I tell you I've drawn you a bath, put your book by the tub, and hung your most comfy jammies on the back of the bathroom door. When you go into the bathroom to hop in the tub, you are greeted by the glow of your favorite candles. Your book is there as promised.

After some time, I call in and say that dinner is ready. When you come out, the table is nicely set and one of your favorite meals is served. I suggest that you take a minute or two to start eating and then we can talk about work.

I begin our conversation by saying something like, "How did it go? I'll bet you were wonderful." We begin our talk, and I ask all the appropriate questions. I listen as you tell me about your day. It is getting late when we finish dinner and our talk. I say, "If I don't clean this up now, you probably will tomorrow, and it will be a bigger mess. You go to bed. I'll clean up and be there in a minute. I love you to pieces; you are the best."

I come in and you're reading your book. I hop on the bed. I don't get in the bed. I put my arm around you and cuddle you and say I know how tired you must be. I lie by you until you fall asleep.

What are my chances of you being available for physical intimacy tomorrow?

My guess is, most of us would reply that the chances were perfect. In every case, when I share this story, both men and women have some very emotional responses.

There are a great number of lessons in this little scenario. The most important lesson I think we can learn is that the husband's love was not a purchase. There was no motive but appreciation and love. Whatever happens with this couple will be a continuation of this gift of love. If physical intimacy is not expected but flows as a natural consequence, it is not a payment of an invoice or bill. It is appropriate. A natural response to kindness is generally kindness. A natural response to interest is interest. This man was interested in his wife. How do I know? He knew what she was reading. He knew she liked candles, even which candles. He knew what a favorite dinner was for her. He asked about what was important to her. If he did these things, would it not be natural for her to feel closer and more available to him?

Our natural tendency is to respond. We want to give back by responding in kind to what we have received. Sometimes that can be a negative thing. When someone is unkind, our tendency is to be unkind back. We learn two things by understanding our tendency to respond. First, we don't have to respond if we choose not to. In an example of being treated unkindly, we make great effort to be better and not respond similarly. Second, as long as we have this responsive nature, we can choose to use it in a good way.

Our lives change when we decide to be kind to each other. Our lives change when we decide to be kind to ourselves. Kindness, like anger and the other strong feelings we have, both positive and negative, changes everything it touches. That is why it is desirable to continue in kindness, even if it's not being returned. In choosing to give a good gift to those around us, even if it is not reciprocated, we choose the better part for ourselves. One woman goes away for the weekend and her husband thinks, "She doesn't love me; she doesn't want to be with me." Another woman goes away for the weekend and her husband thinks, "Good for her. She really deserves a rest; she's been working so hard." Still another woman goes away for the weekend and her husband thinks, "I'll miss her, but I'll have time with my boys." We take control of how we experience our lives by choosing our responses to what life sends our way.

If what I am doing is what I have chosen to do, it feels great. When I'm not worried about getting any specific response, I am not dependent on someone else to give me value or lift me up. I am giving a gift when I love. I give the same kind of gift whenever I do any good thing of my own free will and choice.

"And thus they should impart of their substance of their own free will and good desires towards God . . ." (Mosiah 18:28).

"Verily I say, men should be anxiously engaged in a good cause, and do many things of their own free will, and bring to pass much righteousness;

"For the power is in them, wherein they are agents unto themselves. And inasmuch as men do good they shall in nowise lose their reward" (D&C 58:27–28).

Kindness is a choice we can make. It has an effect on us. We see it reflected in the eyes of those who have already made the decision to be kind. I knew a man who exemplified kindness. We talked one day about whether our lives would really make a difference in the world. He said, "Mine won't." He went on to describe how common he was. He explained, "I don't have a fortune to leave my kids or to charity. I have worked hard and tried to do a good job, but so does almost everybody. In fact, I have a little bet with my wife. When I die, there won't be many people at the funeral. I predict the middle section of the chapel will only be half full at most."

I took exception to his comments. He was a good man who had helped countless people over the years. What he just did as the "right thing to do" was stellar service. He thought nothing of it. He dismissed my objections to his comments as the foolish ramblings of a kind friend. "Wait and see," he said.

I was the bishop when he passed away. I presided at his funeral, where those who came to pay their respects filled the chapel, the overflow, and more.

That is one of the reasons God gave us agency. He knows that our giving without need or expectations frees us to enjoy giving a good gift. He knows it makes us more grateful for what we receive. He wants us to have the great joy He has. He wants us to become more like Him.

The resolve to help others comes from feeling the joy that real love brings. My guess is that most of us would have very little trouble remembering with fondness times when we gave without the need to be recognized or rewarded. The joy that comes from genuine love and kindness is as lasting as it is strengthening.

One example that comes to mind is a Christmas when we decided as a family to concentrate less on gifts for ourselves and more on giving outside the family. We shopped for Christmas groceries and left bags and bags of wonderful holiday treats on porches where the girls would ring the bell and run. The joy we felt in the car driving from house to house is something we talk about now, more than twenty years later, as one of our favorite Christmas memories. Such is the power of choosing to love.

The Joy of Abandoning Scorekeeping

When we stop keeping score and begin just giving, it cleans up a lot of things. We save all the energy we were using to figure out why somebody was doing something. We can forget about who's ahead and who's behind. We don't have to wonder what we owe and what we should have done. When we have a speck of faith and a bit of trust, it might even turn into real happiness.

If I lay aside the scorekeeping, it means that I can give love and service by choice, not out of guilt or obligation. It means that I can feel good even if I don't know when I'm going to get mine. It means that I can graciously receive, not worrying about what I will owe.

I believe that God has invited all His children to come and live with Him again. I also believe it is our choice to respond to that invitation or not to. It is up to us.

When we understand and accept that we get to make our own choices and that others will make theirs, we are relieved of so much baggage and guilt. If we really believe that having a relationship as a friend doesn't obligate our friends to do what we want them to, we are freed from the responsibility of trying to control them. How I feel about my spouse, my best friend, my college roommate, or my missionary companions changes in a dramatically positive way if I take responsibility for my choices and recognize other people's right to do the same.

There's a great Buddhist story about the power of choice. This is a familiar Zen Buddhist parable, so there are many different versions of it. I tell it this way:

There was once a great swordsman who had become a teacher of the truth as well as the sword. He was very old but was still a master with the blade.

One day, a young challenger looking for a reputation as a swordsman arrived in the village and challenged the old master to fight. He knew that if he could be the first to defeat the teacher, he would be a famous warrior. It was with this hope that he challenged the old man.

The young challenger had the special ability to spot and exploit any weakness in an opponent. His opponent's first move would reveal a weakness. He would then strike with amazing force and lightning speed. He had won every match he had been in by exploiting the very first move of his opponent.

With an understanding of the challenger's reputation, and against the counsel of his pupils, the teacher agreed to the challenge. As the two prepared for battle, the old warrior assumed a comfortable attitude and, with his sword in the ready position, simply waited. The young warrior began to insult the old man. He spat on him and challenged his manhood in every conceivable way. He abused him with every curse and insult one could imagine. But the old warrior just stood, still comfortable with his sword in the ready position and a very slight smile on his face.

After a long time, the young warrior was exhausted. He knew he was beaten and sank slowly from the courtyard in shame.

Some of the students and other onlookers were disappointed that there had been no battle. Others were just curious and questioned the old and now-victorious warrior. "How could you allow such insults? How did you win without a single blow?"

The master swordsman and teacher considered the questions carefully and responded with a question of his own: "If someone offers you a gift and you do not receive it, to whom does the gift still belong?"

The old master in this story was unconcerned about what others thought about him. What mattered to him was being true to himself. And thus he won the victory.

Learn to be comfortable with who you are. That is the way to get over the habit of keeping score. Stand quietly, and just be true.

Conclusion

The skills and concepts discussed in this book will help us live our lives with less regret. That doesn't mean there won't be challenges or sorrow. Applying these principles doesn't mean life will be perfect. The objective is to learn and grow and get the most out of our lives.

There are more good things to do in a day than anyone can do. I remember working hard as a bishop to get as much done as possible. For the most part, everything I did was a good thing. But at the end of every day, my to-do list was always full of more good things.

It is a form of perfectionism and arrogance to feel bad that you can't do everything. Nobody can. The only solution I can see to this dilemma is making a realistic choice about what you can do. Putting too much on the "What is required list" is as damaging as not thinking that anything is valuable. Satan doesn't care why you are depressed and exhausted; he just wants you to get there and stay that way.

Making righteous decisions about how we will use our time is up to us. We can evaluate, choose, and act. That is how we learn. We don't have to be excessively rigid. Thankfully, we can adjust how we use our time if there is some valid reason to adjust. However, in the interest of time and mental health, once we have considered a decision and made it, we don't need to spend a second on whether our mother or Aunt Clara thinks that is what we should be doing.

Be confident. You will make a wrong call now and then. Join the club. You may decide to be the first perfect PTA president in the world. Then you realize that the time away from home required to do that is too high a price to pay. Live, evaluate, learn, and adjust.

I promise that you will get more of the things that matter done, and done well, if you don't spend a moment on the senseless drama of guilt. Trying to do everything all at once or trying to please everyone will just make you tired, and you can't do it anyway. Trying to do it all and flawlessly will make you crazy.

Abraham Lincoln knew the futility of trying to please everyone. The familiar story of the man, the boy, and the donkey was supposedly one of his favorites:

Long ago, in a rural village, a man decided to go to the market and buy some flour. He put a harness and a pack rack on his donkey and started to leave. His young son begged to go along, and he agreed.

They hadn't gone far when a young couple rode by and censured the man for child abuse because he was not letting the little boy ride the donkey. He lifted the boy onto the donkey and started on.

They had not gone far when an older couple rode by and told the man he was foolish to spoil his child. They said he should ride if the boy got to. He climbed aboard, and they went on with the man and the boy on the donkey.

They had not gone far at all when a group of people walked by and chided the man for abusing the mule because both he and his son were riding.

The man was confused and perplexed. He wanted to please everyone. They were coming to a bridge when he came upon a solution. He and the boy dismounted, and he shoved the mule off the bridge.

I love this example of the madness caused when we try to please everyone. That way of living our lives and making our choices always proves ineffective and wasteful.

If we are to live lives beyond "if only," we need to recognize how important it is to discover good things every day.

I remember an evening in early July on the lower Nushagak River in Alaska that changed my life. My friend Hank and I were fishing, and it had been a stellar day in every way. We had caught a lot of fish. We had seen eagles, moose, bears, and caribou. It had been a beautiful day, and because we were so close to the Arctic Circle, it was still light outside at 11:30 p.m. We were making our last few casts and discussing the gloriousness of the day as we waited for our guide to pick us up and take us back to camp.

That day was everything a wonderful day in the great outdoors should be. We sat on the side of the river, and our conversation drifted to spiritual things, to the important and valuable things of life and how grateful we were to be alive.

In that moment of peaceful gratitude, I came upon an insight that changed my perspective on life forever. I realized that every day and environment provided something miraculous. I only had to notice it. This may have been obvious to others, but it had not been to me. I realized that how I looked at things had a huge impact on what I saw. I wanted to see things every day that would give me the same miraculous feeling I had that night on the Nushagak.

That changed my life. I decided I would prepare myself to see the miracles in each day, and as a result, I saw amazing things around me. I started to look for the wonder in my world, and the world became wonderful or perhaps wonder filled.

I noticed the camaraderie of good people to work with, the opportunity to have a job that allowed me to provide for my family and do good work. I have a house and a car that runs much more than half the time. I noticed the gospel of Jesus Christ and the opportunity to be the kind of person I want to be. I made a habit of looking for the miraculous. I realized through that process how many gifts I had to be thankful for. It is joyful for me to go to the library and get whatever books I like to read. It's amazing to get on the Internet and find out about life around the world. I can find out about geography, geology, leather working, American history, world history, how to identify birds in the field, all with just a few clicks of a mouse. Even on the most mundane of days, there are countless things at our fingertips that are miraculous if noticed.

Since that day on the Nushagak, I have tried every day to find the miraculous. The best part is, I found and continue to find more than I imagined could be there. I woke up to the reality that I could choose how I saw the world. I know now by experience that how I see the world is up to me, and that knowledge has made an incredible difference.

We are miracles waiting to be seen for what we really are. The way to get this perspective is to choose to see each other as Father sees us.

How do we choose to see ourselves and others as Father sees us? The old story that follows teaches that we are not the first ones who need to be taught how to see:

Word spread across the countryside about a Holy Man who lived in a small house atop the mountain. It would be a blessing to receive any teaching he might share. A man from the village decided to make the long journey to visit the Holy Man. It was a difficult trip, but he kept going, knowing in his heart that it would be worth it.

When he arrived at the house, he was surprised at its size. The Holy Man's house was indeed simple. The pilgrim approached the house and saw an old servant sitting beside the door. The old servant greeted him at the door. "I would like to see the wise Holy Man," he said to the servant. The servant smiled and led him inside. The man from the village looked around eagerly as they walked through the house. It was a very small house, so he anticipated that his encounter with the Holy Man would come soon. Before he knew it, he had been led to the back door and escorted outside. He stopped and said to the servant, "But I want to see the Holy Man!"

"You already have," said the old man. "Everyone you may meet in life, even if he or she appears plain and insignificant, has something to teach you. You must see each of them as a wise Holy Man. If you can see people this way, then whatever problem you brought here today will be solved."

If we treat everyone around us as if we could learn something from them, it would change our perspective. We might even recognize what we are capable of, too.

I want to share a story with you that was a wonderful learning experience for me. A couple of years ago, I was alone in the front room with my granddaughter. It was around Christmastime, and I was enjoying a quiet moment with her. I assumed that because she was sitting quietly playing with her doll, it would be okay to start up a little grandfatherly communication. I was wrong.

I started to speak. I said something like, "Sweetheart, do you want . . ." It was there that I was called up short. "Grandpa," she said, not even looking up. She raised her arm and gave me the sign to halt. This was not some passive request, mind you; it was the full hand—the crossing-guard, if-you-continue-it's-a-felony hand. I stopped midsentence as directed, and she said, "Grandpa, not right now. I'm being beautiful!"

I didn't know what to do, so I just read the paper and waited. In about five minutes or so, without any outside evidence that the time for being beautiful was over, she raised her head and said, "What did you want, Grandpa?"

How great it would be if I could just close my eyes and be beautiful. My granddaughter didn't say, "I'm being more beautiful than Suzie." No comparison was required because she knows there is enough beautiful to go around. No matter who wants it, there is enough.

My granddaughter made her boundaries clear without offense or apology. What she was choosing to do had nothing to do with me. However, there were no grudges held for my having interrupted her. She didn't forget me. She cheerfully reengaged with me as soon as it was possible for her.

She didn't owe me an explanation or offer an apology. She communicated her intention and the need for my silence as efficiently as possible.

What did I learn? My granddaughter knew she had a choice about what was going on in her life. She was not afraid to define her personal space, both physically and emotionally. She gave her love and received mine, no strings attached.

Most important, perhaps, she is proof to me that most of what inhibits us and causes remorse is learned behavior. We can change. Isn't it amazing that in order to live a life with less regret and come closer to God, we must become more like a little child?

Do you feel that you are not yet perfect at accepting the gift of agency, establishing and maintaining healthy boundaries, and overcoming the destructive pattern of scorekeeping? Me, too. We are on the journey, and as we go, we will get better with experience and effort. Our success will come with patience and practice with self and others.

One of my favorite quotes, from Ralph Waldo Emerson, expresses beautifully the confidence and joy of making and owning our choices, imperfect though they may be:

"Finish each day and be done with it. You have done what you could. Some blunders and absurdities no doubt crept in; forget them as soon as you can. Tomorrow is a new day; begin it well and serenely and with too high a spirit to be encumbered with your old nonsense."

Life's decisions are not all easy, and life's choices are not all clear. That is why experience is so valuable. We must be willing to use our experience and knowledge to protect others and ourselves. There will come a point when hard decisions need to be made. Our confidence and understanding will allow us to make these decisions effectively.

Fortunately, life is a process, not a destination, and we have time to learn and grow and love if we decide to. By understanding that God gave us the right to choose, we can heed the enticing of the still, small voice. By setting and maintaining healthy boundaries in our lives, we can learn to trust. We can trust ourselves, and we can trust God. By avoiding the trap of scorekeeping, we can learn the art of confidence without comparison.

We can choose to live facing forward. That is how we can live a life without regret.

About the Author

Kim A. Nelson, a graduate of Brigham Young University, has a master's degree in counseling from Seattle Pacific University. He served a mission to the Southwest Indian Mission. Kim is the president of Stillwater Connection, a business consulting firm in Bellevue, Washington. He is the author of *The Stillwater Buckskin, If God Loves Me, Why This?* and *Happily Forever After: A Practical Guide for LDS Couples Who Want to Improve, Grow, and Share An Eternal Relationship.* He and his wife, Lois, have two daughters and three grandchildren.